LOVE & POWER

LOVE & POWER

Awakening to Mastery

Lynn V. Andrews

HarperCollins*Publishers*

"As once the winged energy of delight" and "I live my life in widening rings" reprinted from *Ahead of All Parting: The Selected Poetry and Prose of Rainer Maria Rilke,* edited and translated by Stephen Mitchell, The Modern Library, 1995. Copyright © 1982, 1983, 1985, 1995 by Stephen Mitchell. Reprinted by permission of Random House, Inc. and the translator.

"I am living just as the century ends," "Only in our doing can we grasp you," "You too will find your strength," "I love the dark hours of my being," and "It feels as though I make my way" reprinted by permission of Riverhead Books, a division of The Putnam Publishing Group from *Rilke's Book of Hours* translated by Anita Barrows and Joanna Macy. Copyright © 1996 by Anita Barrows and Joanna Macy.

HarperCollins books may be purchased for educational, business, or sales promotional use. For information please write: Special Markets Department, HarperCollins Publishers, Inc., 10 East 53rd Street, New York, NY 10022.

FIRST EDITION

Designed by Elina D. Nudelman

Library of Congress Cataloging-in-Publication Data

Andrews, Lynn V.
    Love and power / by Lynn V. Andrews. — 1st ed.
        p.   cm.
    ISBN 0-06-018646-1
    1. Spiritual life.   2. Conduct of life.   3. Success.   4. Love—Religious aspects.   I. Title.
    BL624.A533   1997
    291.4'4—dc21   97-8458

97 98 99 00 01 ❖/RRD 10 9 8 7 6 5 4 3 2 1

This book is dedicated to my daughter, Vanessa,
who has lovingly taught me about the balance
between love and power

Contents

Prologue:
The Fine Art of Mastery

This we Know:
The Earth does not belong to man,
Man belongs to the Earth.
All things are connected like the
blood that unites one family.
Man did not weave the web of life;
he is merely a strand in it.
Whatever he does to the web,
he does to himself.

—CHIEF SEATTLE, 1852

I never intended to become a "seer," as Agnes calls me. When I met Agnes Whistling Elk, I was looking for a teacher of this time and of this soil. I felt a need to learn about wisdom from a woman of the West. I wanted to make peace with the spirits of this land, and I wanted my own consciousness to be in balance with nature. No one could have been more surprised than I to find where my destiny led me. I thought maybe I would write someday, but certainly I was much too private a person to teach or lecture or lead a school—all of which I have done over the past fifteen years.

As my cup became filled with new vision and knowledge of the life process, my destiny became clear, as it has for so many others. I had no choice but to share my life experiences with those who were interested. How could a person receive a gift of wisdom and not share it? I was filled with such spiritual abundance that it flowed out of me; I could not hold it back. Fortunately, long before I realized it, for my teachers had prepared me well, my life changed completely, as have the lives of many of my apprentices. As a seer, I work with a wide range of people, and I work differently with each person, because we are all unique and need different challenges to grow. The kind of work I do has a strong base in creating mental, emotional, physical, and spiritual health and well-being. After the beginning balancing of these areas, I guide my apprentices into the techniques of higher consciousness. Each person creates his or her own tools for healing: through rattles, paintings, music, movement, prayer, ceremony, and aesthetics. Together we develop intent and will. We work with the power of dreams. We learn about different levels of consciousness and energy flows that exist in nature and the universe. There is no aspect of existence that we don't touch and learn to see. *Seeing* means having the ability to see health and illness in people, and the *seer* creates a wondrous, magical world balanced in body and spirit.

Shamanism, or the art of seeing with which native peoples the world over have related to the forces of the natural world, can also be viewed as a path to power, a path to mastery. The direction of shamanism is changing dramatically as it reaches out to inspire nonnative peoples to incorporate its ancient wisdom. As our world continues to evolve, so do the language and metaphors for describing knowledge. As the waves of the mighty ocean of consciousness swell and recede, the ocean leaves upon her shores new and compelling information for us to sift through and integrate into our own vast body of knowledge.

I was contemplating the true nature of power late one afternoon as I strolled through one of my favorite desert areas. I stopped beneath a magnificent ironwood tree, and when I looked up through its forest of limbs, I spied the cocoon of a monarch butterfly hanging from the elbow of one of the branches. I was transfixed by the light reflecting off the leaves of the tree and at the same time emanating from inside the cocoon itself. The butterfly, the beauty that had been gestating there, was about to be born. Perhaps I would be privy to that moment of extraordinary creation.

I sat on the earth beneath the tree and, gazing through the light reflections, I thought about my work with my beloved teachers, about the shamanic techniques they had taught me over the years that honed my skills as a seer. The world is indeed changing, I reflected. And the language that we use to communicate our thoughts and to connect with others can become an instrument of constriction and limitation. We often use idiomatic expressions that are particular to a limited group of people within our profession. Attachment to the words we have used to help us become conscious, the very same words that once provided a bridge from one world to the next, such as *power* or *astral projection,* can one day come to work against us, becoming a fence around our consciousness, something that prevents our communication with others.

As I sat watching the emerging butterfly, I realized that I, too, was being reborn from a chrysalis of my own creation. I had formed my chrysalis from certain techniques and particular ways of presenting myself to the world as a contemporary seer. Now they had become such an integral part of my being that a perfect merging of apprentice and teacher had taken place inside my own cocoon.

I looked above me and saw that the chrysalis in the tree was beginning to tear itself open from the inside. In a few days, its transformation would be complete. A brilliantly colored winged butterfly would emerge, having metamorphosed from an earth-bound, colorless creature.

So it is with me and many of my apprentices. I have watched the courageous people with whom I have worked as they applied the techniques I taught them, as they opened their hearts in love, transformed their lives into works of art, and took flight on wings of power. One of these was Jennifer, who left a life of abuse and remarried someone who adored her. Another was Betty, who balanced her empty computer job with a new life as a fine artist. Yet another, Jackie, is now creating a medical practice that also serves as a spiritual renewal center.

We are all changing; we are all becoming more of who we already are. Those of us who face the challenge of integrating the old ways of expression while releasing the old language and familiar symbols will discover new ones—wings with which to fly into higher and more evolved realms. This work will surely benefit the evolution of our own souls and the collective experience of life itself. Expressing this is my task and my gift as I present this book to you. The feeling and ideas arise from the same place wherein my soul has always resided; the language and the metaphors are a brand-new expression of the lightness of my spirit. Come travel the path of true love and true power. Come join me in my flight.

How to Approach This Book

There is a way to read this book that I think will make it more powerful for you and more accessible. I have taken ideas that I feel are most important in each chapter and put these thoughts in italics. These are ideas that are important to meditate and concentrate on in your life. When you come to a paragraph or lines that are set out in this way, simply know that these are truths that need more of your attention.

When I italicize a thought, it means that these ideas have been of special help to me in my life; they have, perhaps, changed my life forever. In my sharing them with you, I am also sharing what I did with these thoughts myself. Take, for instance, the statement: *For power to be present in your life, you must make a place inside you for power to live.* This is a thought that has many dimensions or aspects to it. You can approach this thought from the way you experience your physical life, from where power lives physically within you. You can approach it from the emotional part of you, asking: How do I emotionally feel about power? How do I allow power inside me? Am I afraid of it? Am I afraid of what it means to take my power? Spiritually, how to I feel about power? Do I feel that only God deserves power and I don't? Mentally, how do I think about power? Mentally, is power something that I even understand? When I think of power, do I think of power over someone—manipulation? This is the type of thought process and exploration of ideas that you will need to consider in relationship to the concepts presented throughout the book.

The sacred wheel is a paradigm for the process of mind that helps me in my life when I think about abstract concepts. Take a very simple sacred wheel, divided like the compass into four directions: You have physicalness in the south of that wheel, transformation and emotions in the west, spirit in the north, and mind in the east. If you go around that wheel with every concept or problem that comes to you—starting with physical-ness at the south, and continuing around the west, north, and east—you will find that life becomes more understandable and more accessible, particularly thoughts about issues that are abstract. Oftentimes, we hear a truth that someone else has divined, but how do we make that truth part of our own dream, our own life? I have written this book in the way that I have to make these concepts as accessible to you as I can make them.

I wish you success, power, and love on your journey.

WAYS TO APPROACH KEY IDEAS IN THIS BOOK

1. Starting with the south of the sacred wheel, ask yourself: Am I physically proud of myself? How do I feel physically about spirit?

2.   At the west of the sacred wheel, ask yourself: Do my emotions rule me? How?

3.   At the north of the sacred wheel, ask yourself: Do I bring spirit into my everyday life? How?

4.   At the east of the sacred wheel, ask yourself: Do I think I am my mind? Why?

5.   How can you integrate all these aspects as you hold the key idea of balance and wholeness? List three ways you think you can make a beginning.

Introduction:
A Divine Balance of Body and Spirit

If you want to discover Eternal Life
And live in the radiant desert of Detachment,
Advance bravely on the Path, fearing no pain or loss,
Take each step authentically, risking your whole being.

—ANDREW HARVEY, *LOVE'S GLORY: RE-CREATIONS OF RUMI*

My friend Linda had been a talented and successful architect for many years. One day, she arrived at my house and collapsed into tears of exhaustion. She thrust a piece of paper into my hands—a page she had ripped out from the September 1995 issue of *Architectural Digest*. She sobbed inconsolably while I read a quote on the page by renowned architect Daniel Solomon: "I like to claim membership in a cadre of resistance fighters, a jolly band whose mission it is to attack the ooze that is engulfing the world at the end of the twentieth century. The ooze is a pervasive, invasive disease that operates at every scale—nondescript rooms in forgettable buildings on faceless streets in nowhere subdivisions in non-towns sprawled over obliterated landscapes."

I finished reading and looked at her questioningly.

"I can't stand it anymore, Lynn," she moaned. "I'm part of that ooze. I studied all those years to be an architect because I wanted to contribute something of beauty to the world. But I never have a chance to do my art. I have to spend all my time finding the funds to pay inflated construction costs, and it seems like all people want these days are tract houses anyway. One more little pink stucco wedding cake just like the house next door. And I have no life," she wailed. "I've focused everything on my career, and now I have no fun and I don't make any money either. There's no love in my life!"

I understood her dilemma. At the beginning of her career, Linda had been happy, eager to use her magnificent gifts, and grateful for finding a creative career she felt she could truly love. "You used to have not only technique in your craft, which is your power; it was also balanced with love of your art," I told her. "This is the formula for happiness. Remember how good it felt?"

She nodded with tears in her eyes.

"As the years went by," I continued, "your focus on technique and power, or your drive to be world renowned, increased, while your dedication to the love of architecture diminished. That's why you're suffering. You got out of balance because you abandoned your greatest love, your art form. You have a broken heart."

The imbalance in Linda's life seems to echo a common lament from powerful people in all walks of life. In the years since 1980, when I first started working with people spiritually, I have met with thousands of men and women. Although most were quite successful in a variety of arenas, many of them felt that something essential was missing. They had all focused heavily on perfecting their craft, concentrating on gathering technique and power, but they had neglected the importance of love.

Perhaps they had found a kind of love, a fleeting experience of connecting briefly with another human being, but it was a flash of ecstasy that quickly slipped through their fingers. Even among those who had married, many spoke about a prevailing and omnipotent emptiness, a void that somehow overrode their social, sexual, and physical experience of what they thought was love. Overall, most of my clients seemed to feel that their sense of power and their sense of love were forever out of balance.

The answer to this common modern dilemma lies in the pursuit of mastery, a balanced state that can only exist when love and power walk hand in hand. Mastery is never static. Rather, it embodies a state of flow, an energetic dynamic, forever in motion. It entails the art of gliding forward, much like being a circus performer on a high wire. To continue moving, one step flowing smoothly into the next, is the only way to keep one's balance. To stop is to fall. Imagine a beautiful woman in a sequined costume and pink ballet slippers stepping out onto a thin wire hundreds of feet above the ground. Her right foot is power; her left is love. Mastery lives along every inch of the wire. Equal and alternating steps, right then left, right then left again, will bring her safely to the other side, to the mastery of whatever she wishes to accomplish. If she takes two steps with one foot and none with the other, she has thrown off the balance, her energy drains out, and she will surely fall into the abyss of emptiness and lack of personal fulfillment.

How did my friend Linda arrive at such a state of imbalance in her life? It was not entirely her fault. Contemporary society has moved away from an aesthetic view of life. It is up to all of us as individuals, therefore, to understand the importance of mastery, to be aware of pursuing it, and to keep both eyes open as we step out on to the insecurity of the high wire, concentrating on balancing the right foot of power with the left foot of love.

If Linda had continued in her state of imbalance, there would have been no way for her to find an entry into mastery, and her personal happiness would have remained forever elusive. But Linda chose to take responsibility. Once she understood the source of her deep grief, she decided to be courageous. She joined forces with two other women who were in much the same predicament. Together, they risked their personal and financial security to open their own architectural firm. That was several years ago, and today they are quite successful, specializing in energy-efficient homes that cater to a more aesthetically oriented clientele. Linda's love of her work has returned and, with each passing day, she is moving toward a finer mastery through balancing her two greatest passions, the power of her architecture and finding love and fulfillment in her personal life.

A similar challenge faces each one of us. I have written this book to share with you what I have learned about the fine art of mastering the balance of love and power as we continue our journey here on earth. For some of us, this might mean re-creating our entire career; for others, adding creative projects to the time we spend outside our paying work. But for most of us, some shift is needed to bring us into alignment with our true power.

TWENTIETH-CENTURY SEERS

As a seer, I was able to help Linda see her imbalance and work to transform it. What an apocalyptic concept—to be born as a seer in the twentieth century. I have been able to see lights around people, to see disease in their bodies, to see their pain and their joy since I was a very small child. When I realized that being able to see made me different, separate, from everybody else, even more so than I already felt, I closed down huge pieces of myself and gave them away for what I thought was a better concept.

This was the concept of fitting in, of being part of the norm. When I think of the ancient seers, the wizards, the great shamans, the gurus who have existed throughout history, all words seem inadequate to describe such beings of wisdom—teachers, masters who can change your terrors and your feelings of insignificance into freedom and serenity and wisdom. As Deepak Chopra has written in *The Way of the Wizard* and as so many great magicians have claimed, the world of the seer is the world of alchemy. Symbolically, it's the shifting of gross metal, gross matter, into gold. Gold is the experience of spirit within yourself. It is the state of mastery. It is the final realization that you are one with God, whoever your god is.

As a seer of the twentieth century, you are faced with a most interesting dilemma. You realize that human beings, by and large, are in pain, yet they are terrified of change. They cannot bear the thought of living within the mystery. What does that mean? That means that living in that place of wonderment is within us, that place of the unknowable. That place where magic and mystery dwell scares us. Magic and mystery, if you define the terms (which are really undefinable, but we can approach the heart of it), are places of truth inside your own consciousness where all things are possible, where pain becomes a challenge and a teacher, instead of a horror in your life. These areas become a place where, when you see something new, an illumination on the horizon that brings radiance into the darkness of your own soul, you celebrate and do ritual and ceremony. You don't run and hide within the darkest corner of your mind or within the great cities of the world.

If you are a seer, you know that the great mystery and power is in everyone. Understanding this is the beginning of your journey home. That's where you finally take the correct fork in the road. Power is in everyone, because all things are created by the Great Spirit. No one is lesser than another or better than

another, although we may have different ways of expressing ourselves.

In my experience, we seem to come around on this earth
many times to learn and to relearn. The importance of this is
that we as human beings are afraid of the great mystery, the very
thing that we are looking for. How is it that we are terrified of
the one thing that we are trying to become? We are trying to
become free and empowered, beings of perfection, and yet, as
we stand at the threshold of that perfection, we sabotage ourselves and destroy our progress. I have looked at this situation
in my own family. I watched my father, a magnificent man born
into an extraordinary family of power, destroy all that was given
him, through abuse of himself as well as of people around him.
He would love with his whole heart and soul, and then he
would turn that love into anger and destroy everything that he
had built. I have watched that scenario over and over again in
my life.

How can you, as a seer, exist happily in this world with all
that you can see? You realize that you are within the world, but
the great magic of existence is also within you. Then you begin
to change. Maybe that is another lesson of power. Each person
learns differently, at a different rate, and in a different way. What
might be a second lesson to one person is the final lesson to
another. But surely, when you realize that you are not separate,
even from those who might try to destroy you, you begin to
learn that all is one, that you are not alone in this universe.
When you truly see that and it becomes a part of you, then you
experience bliss.

I learned very early on in my life about the power of nature. I
realized that in beauty is truth. All around me the magnificence
of nature was my teacher. Through all my early years, the loneliness of my childhood was spent in nature, riding horses and living with animals, seeing my reflection in Lake Washington,

studying it, understanding that somehow in seeing my own reflection, I was seeing the face of my god. I don't mean this in a presumptuous way. I mean that when people see their reflection, they also see their creator. But so often people are blind. How do you tear away those veils of ignorance when people hate you for it? I was faced with the dilemma of how to tell someone honestly what I saw.

I sit in a place that I call the sacred witness, observing the world swirling around me in chaos. And I dance with the shadows, wondering what challenge this life is going to bring me next. I watch the wonder and the beauty of the sun rising up over the mountains at dawn. If you are a seer, you know that all the truth that you have ever searched for is in that light, and you are made of that light. I write about it, I speak about it. And because of the materialistic lessons of this world, one of the first things that businesspeople think about is: How do you make money from this? How do you survive? Then you shift and you change and you search within your soul. You almost lose yourself to someone else's idea of the dream. Then one day, you wake up in the middle of the night, and you hear that wise woman inside you talking, as if she's sitting on a rock high in the mountains. She's laughing at you, because, again, you have been seeing the world through someone else's eyes. You have lost your dream and replaced it with someone else's. You have forgotten why you are alive.

Look at the life of the great Merlin, one of the great seers of all times. Did he reach the multitudes? No, not until long after his life had ended. He passed on to other realms, leaving one apprentice, Arthur, who also eventually passed on, and whose world, Camelot, disintegrated behind him. When I think of that, I am first filled with sadness, and then I remember that old woman, that teacher, sitting on a rock in the mountains, laughing again, saying to me, shaking her head, "Don't get caught in the dream. Remember who you are. Remember who you are with all your heart and all your soul. Because you feel powerless now, don't lose your way, for love is all there is."

Years ago, before I met Agnes Whistling Elk and my teachers, an angel appeared to me. She spoke of my life to come. She spoke of the teachers who would be coming into my life. In her presence, I felt whole. She said that my path would not be an easy one, that I had chosen it and to just accept it. I learned, somehow, from that experience that by accepting yourself, you shift and change the whole of your existence. We are afraid to become what we are trying to become, because we don't love ourselves. We are terrified of becoming that person of power.

Power and love are mates. They live together in deep appreciation and support of each other. Without that marriage, there is no true balance of love and power. There might be power, but there won't be happiness. There won't be fulfillment, and there won't be the joy and freedom that you are looking for.

Shamans have always known this. We have put it in different words, used different archetypes, depending on where we came from, but we have always seen the sacredness, the manifestation of the sacraments within the body and how, by breaking our agreements with the sacred, we become ill. What in the world does that mean? It means that we are made of spirit and we are sacred in this physicalness of life. We have the opportunity to manifest a most beautiful reality, a reality that is never-ending, that is truly immortal, because we are immortal. We are part of the all. We are part of the shaman tree that reaches from this magnificent, magical earth up into the heavens, up into the universe, up into the realm and dimensions of the great masters seated at the round table of God. How do you experience this? You begin by taking one step at a time on the sacred path, whatever that path of heart is for you. You begin by trying to listen, by understanding that miracles are part of our everyday life, that you are a living miracle. Miracles are not just jewels being manifested by a guru in the palm of his or her hand. *You manifest the jewel of your existence with every breath, with every day that you are alive.* That's the beginning.

The great mountains that surround us have a power that lives within us as we live within them. There has never been a time in my life when the mountains haven't spoken to me and healed my spirit. They are the Merlins of my life, and certainly my most favorite place to meet Agnes and Ruby. My teachers are the mountains of the world. I was walking this morning at dawn and watching my feet pressing the pebbles into the earth beneath me. I realized that those pebbles are like mountains in their own universe. All things that we step on, that we ignore, that we take for granted, that we don't even remember are teachers, are part of the bliss of tiny, secret worlds that we are unaware of. *Waken to the power of the simplest aspects of your life and begin to grow.* Open your heart to the balance of love and power in your life.

Ideas to Contemplate

1. Do you see the world through someone else's eyes?

2. Do you feel that your life is a miracle? In what way?

3. Name four small things that influence your life in a big way.

Love
PART I

Love is patient and kind;

love is not jealous, or conceited, or proud;

love is not ill-mannered, or selfish, or irritable;

love does not keep a record of wrongs;

love is not happy with evil, but is happy with the truth.

Love never gives up:

its faith, hope, and patience never fail.

Love is eternal.

There are inspired messages, but they are temporary;

there are gifts of speaking in strange tongues,

but they will cease;

there is knowledge, but it will pass.

For our gifts of knowledge and of inspired messages

are only partial;

but when what is perfect comes,

then what is partial will disappear.

—1 CORINTHIANS 13:4–5

1

The Essence of Love

There are only two ways to live your life.
One is as though nothing is a miracle,
the other is as though everything is a miracle.

—ALBERT EINSTEIN

THE POWER OF LOVE: FOUR WOMEN

I have three special women friends whom I have known since high school, and for me our relationship models the true essence of love. We are able to be both challenging and supportive of one another, because of the deep trust and sense of acceptance we have experienced together over the years.

One summer, the four of us decided to take a short vacation together in Santa Fe, New Mexico. The trees and flowers were in bloom, and we sat outside on the patio under a bright blue umbrella at the La Posada Hotel. We were happy to be together, away from work and all our responsibilities. Over the years, our time together has become one of soul searching, a time when we each receive female support, understanding, and a real sharing of the changes in our lives and of the choices we have made since our school days. We have all gone in different directions. I have become an author and a healer. Patricia is one of the biggest actors' agents in Hollywood, much to her surprise. Jan is a mother and wife of a man who owns a plumbing company. Gwen is a lawyer.

As we sat at La Posada, sipping our iced teas and looking at one another, each of us observed the others' wonderful faces and contemplated the map of time and experience that had been written across our expressions and bodies.

Finally, I said, "You know, I am so proud to know the three of you. You have each done such wonderful things with your lives."

Gwen burst into tears. We were surprised by her emotion. I put my arm around her, since I was sitting next to her, and inquired, "Honey, what did I say?"

She blew her nose into a tissue and took a deep breath. "Well, you know, I am making more money than I dreamed I ever would. It never occurred to me that I was going to be a successful lawyer. I became a lawyer because I was interested in law, because I loved what it meant to uphold what is right and to punish what is wrong. I wanted to help, somehow, to make this society moral. I wanted to mirror that by fighting for what has integrity and vision, in the best way that I could. But it never occurred to me that I would be so busy that I would lose myself in this stressful workaday world. I have dated very interesting men in these past ten years, but I never could give up my work enough to be married to any of them. Now that I'm nearing my fifties, I wonder what I've done, and that's why I'm crying."

She cried some more into her Kleenex, really stressed.

"Gwen, are you frightened in some way?" I asked.

"I guess I feel like a little girl, in a way, in a fifty-year-old woman's body, and I wonder if the party has gone on without me, as if everyone else was invited and I was left at home. Maybe by working so hard toward what I thought my goal was, I missed marriage, I missed having children. Oh, my God, I don't know what I've done."

"*But it's never too late*," Jan said, reaching her hand across the table. "My father died when my mother was forty, and she didn't remarry until she was in her late fifties. You can always adopt children. You don't necessarily have to have children."

"I know," Gwen said, "I've thought about that. But you know, now I don't know how to do it. I don't know how to put myself out there, even to attract someone to become married. I honestly don't know how." With this, she started to cry some more. My heart went out to her.

"Gwen, I understand so well what you're saying," I said. "I've been married twice now. I have my beautiful daughter, whom I couldn't continue my life without, and yet I find myself in a similar position. I'm very driven. I don't do anything without my mind flying off in all directions, spinning off new ways to create activities that will help people. I seem driven to accomplish, over and over again. It's funny, because the people who work for me often say that they feel like they're running after a freight train and can never quite catch it. I suppose that's true. What's happened to me, Gwen, though I don't see this happening to you, is that my body is now rebelling. My body is saying, 'Hey, you need to slow down! You need to pay attention to your personal life.'"

I looked around at the others. "What about the rest of you? Have you felt this as well?"

Jan nodded. "You know, one would think that because I chose to be married, be a householder, and have children, that I have devoted myself to my personal life. And yet, in the first fifteen years of their lives, my three children took over my life, and I gave it to them. I thought this was what I should do, and it was what I wanted to do. Frankly, I look at the three of you, and I wish with all my heart and soul that I had a profession that was mine. I lived through my husband, in a way. My husband is a powerful man. He owns a plumbing company. He started out as just a plumber. How could we know he was going to be as successful as he became! But I helped him get there, and he acknowledges me for that. I don't see my husband very much really. He's gone a great deal of the time. We have companies all over the country.

"At this point I wonder what I'm living for. My life has always involved nurturing. My role was to take care of everyone, and now I realize that I don't know how to take care of myself. I know my husband loves me, but he takes care of me mostly in terms of material things. I regret that I have never achieved any landmark accomplishment. Each one of you has left your mark on the world. If I died tomorrow, my family would miss me, and that would be about it."

We were all in shock at her statement. We had never imagined she felt this way.

"I'm stunned, Jan, because I always thought you were so happy," I said.

"It isn't that I'm not happy," Jan said. "It's that I'm not fulfilled. There's a lack of balance in here somehow. *I have had love in my life, but, you know, I haven't found my power.*"

"In my work," I said, smiling at her, "one of the things I always talk about with the women and the men who work with me is the importance of an act of power. *An act of power is an expression in the world of your true essence.* If you don't have an act of power, you can never really see who you are. I think your act of power, Jan, has been your nurturing ability. It gave you an extraordinary mirror through your happy children and your prosperous life. Now that mirror is changing for you; you've successfully raised your family, and now they're moving on. But is that so bad? You've lived something that the three of us here haven't had a chance to experience. You have accomplished something quite extraordinary. I think that wives today are survivors. Wives today accomplish incredible magic. If they can get their kids through school, just through school, without them being in gangs or on drugs, they've accomplished a lot. So I don't see you, Jan, the way you see yourself. I see you as an incredible, shining example, a light to other women."

"Thank you, Lynn. Maybe I can try to see myself like that. I don't know why I demean myself, but I guess I do."

"Well, I have an interesting thing to add to this mix," Patricia said, our friend the successful agent. "I'll bet none of you even knew this, but I wanted to be a star."

We all looked at Patricia with our mouths hanging open.

"I always wanted to be a star, but look at me. I'm not a pretty woman. I'm not a pretty woman at all."

"I think you're wonderful looking," Gwen said.

"Yeah, right, *handsome*. That's not a beautiful woman. Maybe I could have been a character actress," she said.

"All right," I said, "so go on. I'm interested in what you have to say."

"I have been an agent for many extraordinary people. I have made stars out of almost everyone who has come to me. I took on very few clients and did a very good job for them. Now I look around at my life, and I've got everything I ever wanted. I have a wonderful husband whom I love more than anything in the world. But you know what? I miss the one thing that I really wanted. What I really wanted was to be a star. Isn't that funny? And I probably could have been. But I never gave myself the chance. Now there's a sadness in me, and I don't know what to do about it. I guess, in a sense, there's not much I *can* do. I just go on with my life, but inside I feel this sadness, and I'm afraid it will never go away. The older I get, the further away I get from what I really wanted." Tears welled up in her eyes.

"I can't believe this," I said. "Is it possible that we are all sitting here thinking that we have missed our lives, that we have missed what we came here to do? That can't possibly be. I just can't believe that. But it seems so at the moment. And me, I'm doing the same thing. I'm working so hard that I don't have time for my personal life. I'm trying to change it, but it's so hard to do. It's hard because I love what I do; I have a passion for what I do. When an idea comes up for a book, I want to write it with my whole heart and soul. And yet, there has to be time somewhere to live, to dream, to lie on my back on the earth and stare up at the sky and let whatever thoughts want to enter come. So where are we, my three dear friends? Where are we really in all of this?"

"Well," Gwen said, "perhaps we are at that time of change. We are 'changing women,' aren't we? We are women who are moving toward what Lynn calls 'wise blood,' menopause."

"You know, something is interesting to me," I said. "There is something here about focus. When you focus strongly enough to bring yourself to the place of power that each of us has reached in her own way, you often lose what the aim was in the first place. What do you think? Maybe we lost the simple aim to have a harmonious, happy life, balanced in the male and female energies inside us. I don't know.

"Let's talk for a moment about women who have made it, who have survived healthfully and in relative comfort in a time when the demands of life have been so very stressful for almost anyone in this world. Compared to a few hundred years ago, we live like kings and queens. We are extraordinarily fortunate to be who we are and to live where we live, even with all of our problems. What is it that is at the root of our discontent? Jan, what is it for you?"

"As I listen to all of you, I begin to wonder if I have any discontent at all. We all have forged our lives in our own way. I see that if you focus hard enough to become successful at anything, there are pieces of yourself that are not given attention—that little girl, for instance, that Gwen says she experiences inside herself. I see that she needs to be taken along with you, Gwen, when you go to court. I can see that that little girl inside you wants attention, and I also think she wants time to play. You are making it as a woman in a very male-oriented profession, and you've had to be very tough and carry that male shield most of the time. It must be hard for you, isn't it?"

"Yes, it is," she said. "And it's interesting that you say 'male shield,' because in a sense I put on a male mask when I go out in the morning. I make myself as lovely as I can, but then I put a male mask on over it, because I don't want to approach the world from a sexual standpoint. I want to come as an equal, and be that equal. Sometimes I forget that a man and a woman can be equals, that you don't have to *be* a man to be equal with a man."

"I think most women tend to forget that. I think we try to be a man in a man's world, and in doing that," I said, "we absolutely give away our greatest power. In doing that, we begin to lose our souls."

"That's very interesting," Patricia said. "I don't know that I ever thought about it that way, but I think you're right. Certainly Hollywood is ruled by men, and I'm trying to make it in that man's world, just as you're saying. I guess I put on that male mask in the morning and get tough, too. I don't seem to be tough from my woman's side, if that makes sense." She laughed. "There's a little voice inside of me that I talk to myself with."

"I'm going to interrupt," Gwen said, big tears rolling down her cheeks. "You know what I think it is, what I think is missing? When I read articles in *Cosmopolitan* or other magazines about how to attract men and how to wear alluring clothes and so forth, there's something so demeaning about that. I don't mean this as a sexist, politically feminist statement at all. I'm talking about this in a very human way. What I'm seeing is a lack of esteem for the magnificence of what woman is in this world. For the last twenty-five hundred years, this lack of self-worth has been something to deal with, something that we've been trying to understand, as women, and to live with. Perhaps we have conquered it as much as any women can be expected to do in this period of time. Surely, we have managed to find extraordinary realization of most of our dreams. And yes, there are many dreams left to be realized. Maybe that's why we're all here together—to learn not to demean ourselves, to learn to be who we truly are."

"Now that's an interesting thought," I said. "Okay, Jan, if you could be anybody you wanted to be right now, and could live anywhere you wanted to live, where would you be?"

"We live in Seattle, and it's cold and damp a lot of the year. I used to love that, but now I don't love it. You know where I'd really like to live? I'd like to live right here. I wish I lived in Santa Fe. I wish I could just go home, gather up my lovely things and my husband, and move here."

All three of us chimed in, "Well, then, why don't you?"

Jan's eyes widened, and she thought for several moments. "Wouldn't that be something? I wonder what Hank would say. Maybe it's possible. If I lived here," she said, "you know what I'd do? I'd become an expert in Navajo blankets."

"You would?" I said.

"Oh yes. I have loved Navajo blankets and weaving all my life. You know what I'd do? I'd go out on the reservation, if they'd have me, and I'd learn—I'd learn all about weaving. That's what I'd like to do. I'd like to be a weaver."

"Really!" Patricia said. "I can't believe you're saying that. That's fantastic!"

"Well, Gwen, how about you?" I asked. "How would you be?"

"Off the top of my head," Gwen said, "I'd say that I want to be a judge. But that's not true. I hate the law. No, let me say that again. I love the law, but I dislike what the law has become. I am very distressed by what certain people have made of it. Being a lawyer has become something of a joke. We have become caricatures of ourselves, we lawyers. It takes tremendous integrity to practice fine law, but it is so difficult to do in this day and age. Frankly, I'd like to leave law. And what would I like to do? Oh, I've got to tell you, I'd like to find a mate. I don't know if I want to be married, but I've been going with a man now for a long time, and he's always wanted to marry me. I didn't want to leave my law practice for anyone or anything. But maybe it's time. And do you know what else? I don't want to live in San Francisco anymore; it's changed so much. I've lost my love for that beautiful city, and I had such a romance with it once. Now that's gone, and I don't know quite what to do about it."

"Well," Jan said. "What do you mean you don't know what to do about it? *You can fashion your own life.* Just go do what you want to do. My gosh, you have enough money, don't you? At least for a couple of years."

"Yes," she said, "I do. Probably more than that."

"Why don't you go home, get your guy, and take a vacation? Why don't you go to Hawaii," I said. "That would be wonderful. Go to Hawaii, spend some time walking on the beach, and talk about your life and what you want. Maybe you can rekindle this. Maybe you can make a new direction for yourself."

"I just might do that. But I've got to tell you. We've all got to promise that we will meet again soon and see if we actually carry out these plans we've been talking about."

"Patricia, you've been very quiet. What would you like to do now?"

"For me, always wanting to be an actress, a star, I realize that, in a way, I've resented my clients. Isn't that terrible? I need to make some kind of statement to them."

"I've noticed something about you, Patricia. May I share it with you?"

"Yes, of course," she said.

"I've noticed that, like many women and men, you hold a great deal of power in your throat. Do the rest of you notice how, when she speaks, she strangles the words and doesn't utter them fully?"

"Yes, I've noticed that about myself. It's really funny you say that, Lynn, because I get sore throats all the time, and I find it very difficult, oftentimes, to say what I feel. And you know what's at the root of that?"

We all nodded our heads, because we knew what her words were going to be before she said them.

"I haven't told the truth to myself about wanting to be a star. As a result, of course, if you don't know your own truth, you can't be completely and honestly truthful with others. Women throughout time have not been allowed to express their emotions, yet we feel that we deserve a voice in the world. We have taken our voices of late."

"We have," I said, "but even when we do, maybe it's not the whole truth. It's just part of the truth, because it's so hard to change our conditioning. We shouldn't be so hard on ourselves for that, because we've already done so much. My God, we've done so much! In fact, we should celebrate ourselves."

"Oh yes," everybody agreed. We all held hands and looked at one another with deep love.

"But, Patricia, you still haven't told us what you would like to be doing."

"As I'm thinking here with all of you," she said, "I realize I love what I do. I love helping people become the best that they can be. My problem is that I didn't do it for myself. I'm a really good agent. There's no question about that. I know my business. But now I have to do it for me. I'm just not sure what 'it' is."

"Why don't you take some acting lessons?" I said. "Maybe you have no idea what talent is hidden there. You'll know if you're good or not, and if you're not particularly talented, you can simply admit it and find another act of power."

"I know I have talent, because I acted in high school. Don't you remember? I was in those stupid little plays, and I was good. You know, I never invited any of you, because I was too embarrassed."

"Well, that was ridiculous," we all chimed in.

"Well, it's the truth. But do you know what? I'm going to take some acting classes. If nothing else, I'll just enjoy myself."

"I think what you just said," I said, "is really important. But be careful of something: 'Well, at least I'll enjoy myself.' I think what that means to a lot of women is: 'I'll keep myself busy. It gives me something to do.' There's a great danger in that concept. It isn't good enough just to want to have something to do. What you need is an act of power. You know it, and I know it. You need absolutely to find a way to be a star in your own world. Whether it's being a phenomenal cook, somebody who can wash a dish better than anybody else, or something else. This is one of the first things that my Native American teachers taught me. *Be a star in your own world, whatever that is, but make the effort.* Find the intent and the courage to do it."

"Okay, Lynn, we've been doing a lot of talking here. A lot of wonderful things have been discussed. What about you, kiddo?" Jan asked. "What about you? If you had to do it all over again, would you write all those books? Would you start a publishing company? Would you be a healer? What would *you* do?"

I laughed. "I think I'd raise roses and little baby horses," I said with a big smile. I watched all of them as they watched me, and then said, "I was born with a pencil in my hand. Whenever I wanted to feel good as a kid, I climbed that old apple tree and wrote stories about Spice and Spunk, two little pinto ponies. I wrote poetry or descriptions of the world I saw around me. I always wanted to make people feel better.

"The other day, I took a friend to see a horse, a beautiful Arabian mare and its foal. They were exquisitely beautiful, tender and gentle. I wanted very much to make my friend happy, because she wasn't feeling well. She was disgruntled and unhappy with her life. I thought this would make her happy. Well, as it turned out, this woman didn't think the foal was cute; she didn't think the mare was beautiful. I was crushed. I just couldn't understand it. I was reminded that we all have different aesthetics; we all enjoy different things. The sadness is, we cannot change people; people have to change themselves. That takes a special awareness and a perception of beauty and joy in life around us. If you can't find the joy in a magnificent sunset, or an eagle in flight, or a baby horse with big innocent eyes, if you can't see the beauty, nobody can force you. Something in you has to change in order for you to perceive the aesthetics and take them into your soul and illuminate yourself with the joy of the creation of life."

We all sat for a few minutes, sipping more iced tea. A woman came with more homemade bread, pats of sweet butter, and a bowl of fruit, then walked away, leaving us alone to enjoy the afternoon and the breeze that had come up out of the south, rustling the silvery leaves of the cottonwood trees standing high around us.

"I guess I would do just what I'm doing," I finally said. "I think the only difference is that I'm going to take time—time to dream, time to, as they say, smell the roses. I'm going to take time to take it easy, learn to breathe, and, hopefully, I will get the lesson that's right in front of me. *I have to admit that I think, like all humans, we're in this life to learn something, and we're here*

because we have a blind spot that eludes us. We think we understand so much about ourselves, but all the people around us—
our parents, our teachers, our friends—see what we're missing.
And it doesn't matter if they tell us ten times what we're missing;
we still don't get it. In a way, it gives me a sense of joy. I think
that when you know there is still room to grow, and you have
loving, wonderful friends who share your innermost secrets
with you without judging you, you have tremendous wealth.
Part of that wealth is knowing that we have room to develop and
still become more of what we are. Just being able to realize that,
all four of us, we're beginning to learn the lessons that we came
here to learn. Isn't that what life is about? It's about realizing
that it's not outer gain we're after. Nothing we've talked about
has to do with outer gain. Do you think?"

They all nodded.

"I think it's about what's inside, and that if you're chasing an
illusive exterior 'something,' filling yourself up with the things
and distractions of this extraordinary society that offers so
much, then you've missed the point. You'll never find that blind
spot or be able to open the eye of perception that will be found
there. It's not really that the eye is blind; it's that the lid is closed,
because at the moment it doesn't realize that there is something
to see."

"You know," Patricia said, "that reminds me of a conversation
I had not long ago. I had seen the play *Fences* the night before
and had the wonderful opportunity to share a short time with
the star, James Earl Jones, who was receiving the Tony Award
that year. At one point I asked if he had seen the reviews. He
said, in his thoughtful manner, he hadn't, nor was he interested
in seeing them. I was so surprised. I told him the reviews were
so fantastic I would have thought he couldn't wait to read them.
He looked at me with a very serious face and said that he never
looks at the reviews. I asked him why, and he said because the

reviewers don't understand his art. They don't understand the process he has gone through for all these years in the practice of his craft. When they make a comment, it's always about the end result. He looked at me and said, 'If I were waiting for the critics to give me an accolade, if I were waiting for the effect of my work, for the results to come in, before I knew whether I had done a good job or not, then I would consider myself someone who did not understand the craft of acting at all. I go through a process for months and months before I become a part in a play or film. I start from the shoes on up, and there isn't a critic I can think of at the moment who understands that process. So why would I want to read what they have to say about me?'"

We sat in silence for a moment, thinking about this.

Finally, I spoke up. "As you told that story, I thought about something in my own experience, and I really understand it now. If we wait for the external acceptance of anything we do, we can never become the master of that art, whatever it is, don't you agree?"

"It is really true," said Gwen. "I've been practicing martial arts for many years, and it has helped me understand that it is all in the doing, and if your excitement and thrill about life is not in the doing, then you have missed the point."

"I think it's true, Gwen," I agreed. "I have a dear, wonderful friend who is one of the finest horse trainers in the world today, and yet when I started working with him, I found that because riding came so naturally to him, he didn't know exactly what it was that he was doing. So he found it difficult to teach amateurs. He didn't know why he was so good, so he couldn't explain himself well. If you don't know why you're good at something, how can you feel fed by that activity; how can you feel that you've accomplished anything? I think that's what was happening to my friend. He didn't really understand why he was as good as he was, and as a result, when he lost a class he was very, very angry and upset, as if the winning or the losing were his mark of approval in some way."

"Exactly," Patricia said. "It's as if he was chasing after the external acceptance, and if you have to chase after those externals, you are never going to feel like a winner, even if you're winning."

We continued chatting for a while as the shadows lengthened. As our conversation wound to an end, I was filled with a sensation of profound gratefulness for these women in my life. They have helped me realize that searching for wisdom and self-empowerment is a necessary part of life. Moving forward and peeling away the levels of negative conditioning through communication can bring each individual to mastery. Together, we have realized that this is not a selfish process, but an essential one, a necessary part of the power of love. The mastery of our lives needs to be understood fully. Participating in sisterhood and brotherhood on earth is one way to bring yourself to your highest consciousness and to support others in their growth as well. It is the essence of love.

LOVE AND POWER

True power is love. First let me explain what I mean by power. This is a word whose meaning has been twisted and changed over time. When we speak of power, many people become afraid or uncomfortable. They think of police and tax collectors and others having *power over* them. This is not what I mean by power. *Power, in my way of thinking, is partly the understanding of the spiritual energy that flows through all beings.* This understanding comes from what I call a pulling down of higher guidance into your life—a process of vertical acts of consciousness in which you ascend to the level of spirit and bring back its wisdom, a process which I will elaborate on throughout this book.

Wise people—people who experience balance between body and spirit—can translate that higher energy into healing and transformation for themselves and others.

Power is also the strength and the ability to see yourself through your own eyes and not through the eyes of another. It is being able to place, metaphorically, a circle of power at your own feet and not take power from someone else's circle. What this means is that you have defined your own values and truth, and you live them; you do not try to take your values and truth from someone else.

This book concerns both love and power: two seemingly disparate concepts. As the story of my friend Linda in the introduction indicated, if you do not have love with power and power with love, it is tremendously difficult to maintain happiness in your life.

How do we, as people living under incredible stress, maintain the balance of love and power in our lives? If you have power without love, you may experience moments of happiness, but there's really no way to maintain that happiness. Eventually, you will fall into the abyss of loneliness and emptiness because you have no true intimacy with another person. The reason is simple. *Power without love leaves you without any sustaining energy to keep the feeling of power alive.* Love is what brings power into the realm of mastery, where balance and harmony become an everyday experience. And it is within the realm of mastery that your life becomes balanced, powerful, and magical. You can learn to experience extraordinary brilliance every day of your life.

To achieve a successful balance of love and power, you must establish a relationship with God, Great Spirit, or Source—whatever term you prefer. The key is to avoid the division between matter and spirit that so often confounds people in modern societies. We have our jobs, which are separate from our families, which are separate from our spiritual lives. We have compartmentalized our lives instead of integrating all that we are—as beings connected to spirit. At the heart of a genuine relationship with spirit is a deep and abiding love. This love radiates out from within, allowing us to contact our true power as we express this love and send it outward.

Ideas to Contemplate

1. How do I bring intimacy of thought and emotion into my work?

2. Do I ever consider asking spirit to guide me in my work or my relationships? How?

3. How do I compartmentalize my life?

Loving Yourself

There's another language beyond language
Another heaven beyond heaven and hell
Our hearts live by another heart
What we are shines from a placeless place.

—ANDREW HARVEY, *LOVE'S GLORY: RE-CREATIONS OF RUMI*

Have you ever been in love? You float down the street while everyone is mesmerized by your radiance. You practically glow in the dark. You are full of creative ideas and the confidence to know that you can pull them off. At this blessed time in your life, nothing is impossible. You are Romeo, able to scale ten-foot walls, or you are Juliet, more beautiful than a perfect red rose. How do we maintain this radiance?

You cannot be balanced and harmonious—spiritually, physically, emotionally, or mentally—without feeling worthy of having a happy and powerful life.

To have power has to do with arriving at a goal and still remaining whole as a person—not trading away aspects of yourself that you believe in to please another person or a corporation. If you lose your balance and move out of your center, you may have attained a job or a spouse, but you have lost your soul. *To truly have power, you must first love yourself enough to stay in your own center of truth.*

Once we have embraced love as a feeling about ourselves for ourselves, it will never go away. When we understand that the love we feel is our own—that it is not generated by this man or that woman—then we perceive it differently. It becomes a state of being, not dependent on any other person or thing. It is maintained by the constant awareness of keeping our heart open to ourselves and others.

Ideas to Contemplate

1. Do you love yourself? Your body? Your power? In what ways?

2. Do you feel worthy? List ten things you have accomplished in your life, and celebrate them.

LOVE AND THE ROAD TO MASTERY

Learning to love oneself is the first step on the road to mastery. As in any kind of learning, the modeling and teaching of those who have already achieved a degree of mastery makes all the difference. I would like to illustrate this discussion with a short story.

For many years I have loved horses, and I have engaged actively in showing them. I was working with my horse trainer one afternoon, and I was having a hard time getting my horse to respond in the way that I wanted. My trainer, a very wise fellow, came out of the center of the ring and asked me to stop. He asked me to get off my horse, and he got on.

"I want to show you something," he said. "The difference between a world-class trainer and an amateur is understanding hold and release. Let me show you."

He took hold of the reins and pulled the horse's head gently into position. When he then released his hold, the horse's head remained in that spot without the pressure on the reins.

"The difference between you and me is timing," he told me. "I know when to hold the horse in place, and I know when to release the horse when he has found the right position. Then timing becomes an issue of knowing when to pick up the reins again when the horse is moving out of position. It's a feeling, an intuition you get if your intent is focused. You begin to hold just as the horse is beginning to move out of position, and it's a split-second reaction. You have to learn and understand when to release that horse so that he gets comfort and a reward for moving into the right position."

I'm telling this story because it's hard to explain timing to people who don't have a real sense of it. Timing is something that comes from your gut, from visceral understanding and the ability to sense the right moment to move or to release. To master this technique requires a deep and abiding love of your essential self. When you hold on to a situation in your life, you hold on to it until, perhaps, you have learned what you need to learn in that particular situation. You may have experienced this in dealing with a difficult friendship or job. I think all of life is a schoolhouse. Life is a process of learning, and timing is part of your education. You hold on, and then you release the situation when the moment is exactly correct.

Feeling and understanding this process of timing is not an easy thing, but it is one key to self-love. So often, you tend to release when you should hold, or to hold on to a situation when it no longer serves you. When you do this, you have no chance to gain mastery, because when you don't give yourself a chance to sense the timing of actions, you have no sense of the harmonies of nature and how your body relates to those harmonies. You are most likely trapped in your head, afraid to let go of some fear. That is why it is important for you to understand your fears, move into the center of them, and come out on the other side—not only healed but with less baggage. Then your ability to sense the proper timing becomes strengthened tenfold.

Timing, your ability to know when to hold and when to let go, is one of the essentials of a masterful life—knowing when to move, knowing when to let go of a stock before it plummets, knowing when to release, knowing when to buy, when to hold. If you love yourself, then you can love others and release them as necessary. Letting go of friends and situations is often the hardest task, but often the kindest in the long run. If you can sense when to let go of situations that drain you and no longer serve anyone, you hold the key that unlocks the door to true skill and mastery of the tools of power.

Ideas to Contemplate

1. What are you holding on to that needs to be released?

2. Name two times you sensed a problem coming and did something about it.

3. If you don't feel a sense of timing, learn to meditate, or simply sit in nature, for example in a garden, and identify how you feel and notice every sound that you hear. List eight sounds.

BEING WHO YOU ARE

When you really love yourself, you naturally express who you are in the world. You do not "hide your light under a bushel." Not long ago I was working with a woman who was very special. Janice could do everything well. She was an A student, a fine musician, and an Olympic swimmer, though not a medalist.

Because of her uniqueness, she was beautiful, bright, and smart, but Janice had always felt separate and different in her life. She was an only child, raised by intelligent and intellectual parents who, because of their scientific background and positions in the world, were not social. Janice, on the other hand, had a wonderful quality of being able to move out into society with such a sparkle and sense of humor that people were at once attracted to her. But then, because of her strength and the mirror of perfection that she provided for people, they were often frightened by her and moved away from her. Because of this, I thought of the alpha wolf, who, like Janice, is a born leader.

The alpha wolf does not usually have to prove her position, except by her presence. Occasionally she may be challenged, and then she has to fight. But an alpha wolf is prepared to fight, and because she is prepared to fight, she usually does not have to. This quality has to do with her mettle, the steel that is inside her, holding her up, making her strong, which others sense and respect. Ordinarily, others don't fool with the alpha wolf, unless their antenna is down or they want to steal her power. If they want to steal her power, or if another alpha wolf comes along, then the alpha wolf may have to fight for what is hers.

But Janice, because she was part of this society and feeling very lonely, began to try to become a beta wolf instead of an alpha wolf. She tried to become just a member of the pack, because she didn't know how to accept and love herself as a leader. Janice needed a teacher, someone who had been down these roads before her, to show her the way. In her early years, there was no one to play this role.

In trying to become a beta wolf when she was really a leader, an alpha, Janice became very ill. She developed Epstein-Barr, so she could not function optimally, which was, of course, what she was asking for. Because of the dis-ease in her spirit, she created a disease in the immune system of her body. Then she got carpal tunnel syndrome in her hands. The way I look at the situation, she simply could not handle what was happening to her. She could not handle her own power. Then, because of her discontent and her attempts to become somebody that she was not, even though she was praised for the things she was doing, she did not ever own any of it. She felt that if people really knew who she was, they would no longer love her, which had been her experience.

Here was a woman of power not taking her power—an alpha wolf trying to be a follower. This did not work for her; it does not work for anyone. Janice lacked self-love, so she could not truly live in her power; she could not express herself in the world as she truly was. So how did this beautiful woman heal this self-defeating dynamic so she could live a harmonious, balanced life and still be loved?

There is a blending required in such cases, I believe, and it comes first from love—loving the mystery and existence of the world around you, and knowing that you absolutely can be part of its magic. This process includes loving the simple physical existence of your physical body and loving your worth and your specialness even if that means you are different. Janice learned to expand her heart; she learned to simply love being—not doing, not making a mark, but simply just allowing the beingness of her own spirit and soul. Through movement in dance, deep contemplation in order to heal her wounds, and getting to know her spirit through painting, she stopped sabotaging herself. Then, as Janice expanded her own heart toward a new sense of being, she began slowly to rejuvenate the feeling of loving herself, just loving herself as she was and as she is. Then, suddenly, it seemed to her that being the alpha wolf, being a leader, was simply her rightful state of being. Her false nature, which had been quite aggressive in the past, began to settle down. She realized that she had become aggressive because she couldn't get anyone to listen. The more she argued and tried to tell people what to do, the more they misunderstood her.

Janice began to sit in the center of her truth more and more every day, through meditation, through doing private cere-monies with nature—sitting with a tree, for instance, her back to the tree, sensing the sap moving through the tree and acknowledging the tree for its magnificent existence as a per-fected being on this earth. She realized that a tree can only be a tree, and a tree *is* that treeness with exceptional beauty and strength. As Janice meditated with the tree, simply sitting in silence, honoring its presence, she began to realize the choices that we human beings have. We are born human, but we can act like a tree. We can be aggressive or passive. We can act like a donkey or an alpha wolf. Janice began to appreciate what this degree of choice really means in our lives: When we have self-love, we can choose health, we can choose harmony. A tree has to live wherever we plant it, and it has to do the best it can. But if there is a drought, for instance, most human beings can move to a place of comfort. What an extraordinary gift this really is!

Janice truly began to celebrate her newfound sense of har-mony and self-love. Then she brought in aspects of technique. She became more careful about the way she approached people with her strength and her power. She became more understand-ing of other people's faults and lack of courage. She had come down a trail, at first not recognizing herself, disowning huge pieces of herself, and then bringing the fragments back into the newly created puzzle of her personal being, which gave her a fresh sense of stability and harmony. Slowly, she began to live in balance between her love for herself and her newly acquired skills for expressing that love in the world. She became an impressive example and model of female power and self-love.

Janice is now the CEO of a big corporation, but she has been able to bring her spiritual life into her workaday life. For her this has manifested in a gradual retirement plan for longtime employees nearing sixty-five. She realized the need for expert older employees to work less but with equal respect. She realized that retirement needs are different now than they were, so she is working spiritually and economically with her workforce. She has found the balance between love and power as the expression of the bedrock of her self-love. Now mastery is becoming a bigger issue for her. She realizes that balance is one thing, but finding true mastery entails recognizing the essence of God and spirit within her, so that not only is she in harmony with the earthly aspect of life, but the heavenly as well.

ACCEPTANCE WITHOUT JUDGMENT

Some time ago, a woman named Sarah came to work with me. She ran a bookstore in Washington State, and she was feeling depressed because her business was not doing well. We talked for some time about her approach to her world, her approach to spirituality, and how she felt about things. I noticed that she had difficulty sitting for long because her back was sore. It was so clear to me, and soon became clear to her, that she was backing away from her power. She was having a great deal of difficulty expressing herself and her personal truth. In the beginning of our conversation, it was apparent that she was saying what she thought I wanted to hear. The way she shifted her eyes, I knew she couldn't say what was in her heart. She was afraid of something. Then she told me things I could tell were not her own ideas, which, it later turned out, were really expressions of how her family felt. She had been raised a Southern Baptist and had great difficulty with books about channeling, the process of someone receiving instruction from spirits. It turned out that in her part of Washington, people were very interested in just that, and often came into her store looking for books about this channel or that channel. She not only did not carry the books, but often told her patrons how she felt about the subject. As a result, she was losing business. She was very depressed and discouraged about this, as well as about her disharmony with the community around her. We did a lot of work together, and we found that she was expressing and acting out feelings that did not belong to her. One thing Sarah hated was getting dirty. So we went down to the creek and played in the mud, singing, screaming, and getting her in touch with her emotions.

When Sarah began to release these feelings, which had come from her family of origin, she began to move out of the depression that she had been trapped in for so many years. She began to sit straighter in her chair, and her back felt better. Then she discovered that there had been a voice inside her that had been trying to be heard for a long time, and because of her feelings about channeling, she had never allowed it to be expressed. She had an angel that was trying to reach her. In meditation, she found him and listened. As a result of hiding from her angel, she had restricted all of that energy in her back, which was detrimental to both her business and her health. Whether or not you believe in angels and guardians, I believe each of us can contact higher consciousness and see that form as we choose; for Sarah, the form was an angel. As Sarah began to express her true feelings, and as I listened to her and accepted her without judgment, she began to see that this was how she should be running her business—with acceptance and without judgment. She saw that she should not act as an oracle for her customers, as that was not her position in life. She was running a business that she loved, and she wanted that business to be successful. To accomplish this, she needed to provide a service, to refrain from judging her clientele, and simply to present what was out there.

Sarah also found in this process that she was more open to new ideas than she had ever been. She realized there was a whole world out there. She had unwittingly judged that world negatively, as if she were living inside the skin of one of her family members, even though she had left her family years and years ago. They had been rigid, unforgiving, and closed to new ideas. Sarah desperately wanted to be open to what was new and exciting, but she feared that if she was she would no longer be loved, and might even be punished, so she backed away from herself and possible success. This was her core issue on a very unconscious level. Together, through deep spiritual praying, listening to divine guidance, meditation, and expressing her creativity through writing under my guidance, Sarah released memories she had stored in her body from childhood. Sarah needed to be accepted as she was, and she needed to be loved, as we all do. Finding self-love was the key to her assuming power in her life, and out of her newfound love and power, her business began to turn around. These same principles can work for all of us, and they hold the secret to living our lives out of the powerful wellspring of self-worth and self-love.

Ideas to Contemplate

1. How do you feel about prosperity? Do you feel worthy of it?

2. Are you afraid of new ideas and ways of experiencing reality? Why?

3. What do you think about angels and spiritual guides?

4. Meditate and ask your spiritual guide to speak to you. Describe what you hear.

5. Do you judge yourself? Do you judge others? Consider how to move through these judgments and become open to self-love. List four ways to do this.

3

Loving Others

I thought I had exhausted terror, being trampled
To become Your dust, finer and finer . . .
Then the night came when You whispered "I am you"
And vanished, leaving me everywhere nowhere.

—ANDREW HARVEY, LOVE'S GLORY: RE-CREATIONS OF RUMI

Every relationship in your life provides an opportunity for spiritual growth. Once we can see love as a fluid state of receptivity within our own hearts, then we can send it outward so that it touches all of those around us. Let's compare two kinds of lovers. The first type is a study in technique. He views love as an act of sexuality; he knows all the moves and has practiced them from a mental place. He feels confident in his ability to do the right thing at the right time. But when the physical act is over, both people are left feeling cold and empty. No connection has been made because the main ingredient was left out: love.

The second type of lover is all heart. Overflowing with passion, he views love as a way of life, but this person has no idea how to touch his lover with enough sensitivity that she will be able to receive him. The concept is right, but, once again, no connection is made.

The true archetype of the lover, however, merges technique with an open heart in order to connect with another human being.

THE MAGIC OF LOVE

Loving another is a different experience for everyone, and it may mean several different things to each one of us. For me, I can best describe it as a profound feeling, a stillness in which I sit quietly and ecstatically, basking in the center of a continual flow of bliss.

Love is our savior. It is the force that brings the good things in life to us. When Margot Fonteyn, the prima ballerina of the Royal Ballet of England, was close to forty years old, she was thinking about retiring. She had already danced well beyond the artistic expectancy of a dancer and had had a glowing career. The arrival of Rudolph Nureyev, the young upstart performer, in his twenties, who had suddenly defected from Russia, created a dramatic shift in her plans.

When the two met, it was love at first sight. Not romantic love, but rather a recognition of a deeper love born out of respect and admiration for a shared art form. They joined forces, and the strength of their love allowed Margot Fonteyn to dance at peak performance level for ten more years. It allowed her to express her own unique power.

However you define it, love is something we all want, whether or not we admit it to ourselves or to anybody else. *See your life as a canvas spread out before you upon which you can manifest any reality you want.* You can paint a picture of anything you can imagine, but there is something you must know before you pick up the paintbrush. If love is absent from your palette, your picture will be just that: a picture. In order for it to come alive as an art form, to explode out of two flat dimensions into multidimensional existence, you must come from a place of love.

TO CREATE ART, YOU MUST FIRST HAVE LOVE

I have an apprentice and friend named Carol, who is a brilliant financier. She had mastered her technique, but in doing so, she had become overly identified with it. She was used to manipulating vast sums of money, and she thought she had to be cold and mathematical in her communication in her personal life, just as she was in her work life. When men appreciated her, which happened often because she was hauntingly beautiful, she would turn into an ice queen, becoming cold and unresponsive. This didn't make men feel welcome, so Carol had spent a great deal of her adult life on her own. She came to see me because she had been feeling terribly lonely.

Carol asked me for spiritual counseling, and we worked to find the pieces of herself that she had given away or denied. I felt that these lost pieces would be the key to unlocking the door to her hidden soul and her ability to love. The work was arduous, as her fear and programming made her in certain ways unyielding, but I found her dedication inspiring. She so wanted to break through her armor and feel the vitality of life. We journeyed together into her body through guided meditations and found pain and symbols of caves and places of fear where she held her grief over being an unwanted child. We freed that pain through creating paintings together.

One night, in desperation for a new way to create an opening, I decided to transport our classroom into the arms of nature. I suggested we take a walk down a familiar dirt road in the mountains. Carol was game. When we began walking, I noticed that she kept staring up at the moon, which was hiding intermittently behind the clouds. We stopped at a bend in the road and focused our attention on the sky.

"Those clouds are like the veil that surrounds you," I said to her.

"Yes," she answered. "I am hidden, like the face of the moon."

"What will make the clouds go away?" I asked as we continued to walk in the moonlight.

Carol was silent for a while. I said nothing and breathed in the beauty of the night. "Gratitude," she whispered finally and began to cry. I hugged her and looked into her tearstained face. Carol hadn't cried since she was twelve years old, when her dog died. "It sounds so simple and stupid," she said, "but when I said the word *gratitude,* I felt an opening like a canyon in my chest and stomach. In this moment, I feel truly grateful that I can experience the beauty of nature and the beauty of my own body. I am beautiful, aren't I?" she asked timidly.

"Yes, you are very beautiful in both body and spirit," I said.

Carol had never allowed herself to appreciate her own beauty and abilities and be grateful for them. She had never allowed a wonderful man into her life who could remind her of her specialness. She had never loved another because she didn't feel lovable within herself. She had been too afraid to love—until that night, walking under the obscured light of the moon. Carol became close to her God that night, and she felt grateful for that God-like presence inside her. Carefully and slowly, she began to open to the experience of love with another person. She began to make of her life a work of art by balancing a newfound feeling of love and appreciation for herself with her power.

When we have been closed down for most of our lives, it takes time to open up. For Carol, learning to love herself entailed the reassembling of various pieces of herself that she had disowned, such as her sensitivity, her creativity, her humor, and her beauty. Through this process, she began to feel worthy.

If we imagine love as the dream come true that lies within each of our hearts, then expressing that love is giving voice to the yearnings that have always been there. So it was for Carol.

Ideas to Contemplate

1. Are you afraid of being loved? Why?

2. Are you afraid of becoming what you are trying to become? Why?

3. How does your level of self-worth affect your ability to love others?

THE GIFT OF LOVE

There is yet another dimension to loving others, one demonstrated to me quite powerfully by my teacher, Agnes Whistling Elk, one afternoon as I stood shivering in terror at having to speak in front of a large audience. I am by nature a shy person. Agnes said something to me that I have never forgotten: "But, Lynn, you love to give gifts, don't you?"

"Yes," I replied.

"Well," she said, "you have received many gifts of learning from us, so when you approach an audience, look at it from a different place. You implode your energy when you become frightened. Think of moving that energy out, and think about giving those people a gift of your wisdom and understanding."

Just those simple words changed so much in my life. I came to see public speaking as an act of love, a true giving of myself. I had to learn to teach in front of groups of people if I was to share the gifts I had been given, and realizing this was one of the greatest and most expanding lessons of my life. *I realized that you can feel and express love in many ways, not only to one special person, but through your love of God, your love of the soul of humanity, and your love of doing and giving.*

I also had to learn to think in terms of somehow supporting myself, and I had to learn to understand the exchanges of energy that occur when you put forth effort, for instance, to teach a person who comes to you for guidance. You need to receive energy back in some form in order to live, as well as to break the energy cords that are created by working with someone. That was a very difficult thing for me to deal with. I realized that if I were working in a cabin in the far north of Canada, I might want food in exchange for my services, because that is what I would need to live. But if I were living in Los Angeles or New Mexico, I would need money to pay the rent. It became apparent to me that money is the trade beads of the twentieth century, and I would need energy in the form of money in exchange for my services. This was another great lesson along my path toward integrating love with power.

Not only did I recognize the need for loving what I do, but I learned to release a deep passion for communication with others. I found that, yes, money was involved to help sustain a physical flow, but that it all became a totality of effort and response. Each part—the ideas, communication, effort, commitment, self, God, and response—became the sum of a much greater whole. It's not about money and accomplishment really. It's about the manifestation of love.

Ideas to Contemplate

1. Describe three ways you communicate your love to someone.

2. Do you need love or want love?

3. Do you feel uncomfortable accepting money? Why?

THE KEY TO LOVING OTHERS

The true key to loving others is recognizing that sharing abundance is part of your growth toward self-realization. Truly, giving to others is giving to yourself, and loving others is not possible unless you love yourself.

A sense of abundance, of more than enough for all, resides in a grateful heart. You can create gratefulness in your heart with vertical acts of consciousness, where you communicate with God through prayer, appreciation of beauty, or even a walk in nature. These acts enable you to reach up and bring down into your being a sense of spirit and the mystery of life. Then the flame of spiritual and physical abundance will burn within your will and give you radiance, as you grow toward self-realization.

Self-realization is not the laying on of more ideals, more rules, more knowledge. It is the understanding that you can truly live a life of consciousness and freedom. It is partly the stripping away of the activities in your life that no longer serve you. It is the discarding of conditioning that bleeds away your energy, as the story of Carol illustrated. Then the important things in your life can receive the strength and energy they need for their completion. You are like a battery. You save energy and you use energy every day. Use it wisely, so that when you come to difficulties and situations that require extra power, you will have it.

Ideas to Contemplate

1. How do you waste your energy? How does this affect what you have left to give to yourself and to others?

2. Name two situations that no longer serve your growth. What could you do to change them?

Loving others begins as a process of reaching across the boundaries that separate people and opening yourself to a true oneness of spirit where experience is shared, where you meet kindred souls moving through lives not so different from your own. *Once the gateways to all possibilities have opened, your life will be filled with extraordinary shifts and changes.* You and your loved ones will be able to let go of old situations and old relationships that no longer work, and move on to newly structured lives. Listen well and love well; the answers to your questions are all around you.

Ideas to Contemplate

1. Do you believe you are worthy of change? In what ways?

2. What activity (or activities) is (are) bleeding away your energy? What will you do about it?

*P*ower

PART II

Before the land of Egypt rose out of the waters at the
  beginning of the world, Ra the Shining One came into
  being. He was all-powerful, and the secret of his power
  lay in his Name which was hidden from all the world.
  Having this power, he had only to name a thing, and that
  thing too came into being.

"I am Khepera at the dawn, and Ra at noon, and Tum in the
  evening," he said—and as he said it, behold, he was the
  sun rising in the east, passing across the sky and setting in
  the west. And this was only the first day of the world.

When he named Shu, the wind blew. The rain fell when he
  named Tefnut the spitter. After this he spoke the name of
  Geb, and the earth rose above the waters of the sea. He
  cried, "Nut!"—and that goddess was the arch of the sky
  stretching over the earth with her feet on one horizon and
  her hands on the other. Then he named Hapi, and the
  sacred River Nile flowed through Egypt to make it fruitful.

Then Ra went on to name all the things on earth, which grew
  into being at his words. Last of all he spoke the words for
  "Man" and "Woman," and soon there were people
  dwelling throughout the land of Egypt.

After this Ra himself took on the shape of a man and became
  the first Pharaoh of Egypt.

—"Creation Myth," *Tales of Ancient Egypt,*
  translated and edited by Roger Lancelyn Green

4

Possessing Power

I am living just as the century ends.
A great leaf, that God and you and I
have covered with writing
turns now, overhead, in strange hands.
We feel the sweep of it like a wind.
We see the brightness of a new page
where everything yet can happen.
Unmoved by us, the fates take its measure
and look at one another, saying nothing.

—RAINER MARIA RILKE

THE DRY CREEK BED

I was sitting in the sand on a flat sandstone rock on a cliff in the high desert of Arizona. My friend, a wise old Indian woman, her hair wrapped in a red bandanna, was sitting beside me. The wash before us was barren sand and a tumble of large rocks surrounded by half-dead mesquite and palo verde trees.

"Not much different than the world these days," my friend said wistfully, indicating the wash with a stick.

"Somewhat," I said.

"What do you mean?" she asked.

"Well, this dry creek bed reminds me in some crazy way of power. There is great power and strength in these rocks. And the sand holds memories of ancient storms, the silent relentless gravity of glaciers, and the explosions of ancient volcanoes filled with fire and power. But look at it all now, like the slow disintegration of a great society or a great icon of power gone bad. What went wrong? When did the decay begin? Was it just age or change?"

"It comes from loss, not gain," the old woman said, her face lined with weather and time like the rock beneath my hand.

"Yes, my friend, so many great men—Jung, Plato, Nietzsche— so many have written and thought about power. *What about woman and her dream of power and love? Have we lost her?* Because she was here once. She wrote of the balance of power and love through the sap in the trees, the heart of the horse, the eye of the storm, and the balance of nature," I said with tears in my eyes.

"I think we feel her here in this land."

"Yes, and what is missing in the books about the art of war and power is the movement, as the flowing water brings back memory and life to this river bottom. It's the life-giving water, the nurturing love of Mother Earth—her blood—that's needed. It's love that animates us all. We as human beings can translate nature in many ways—we make houses out of trees, walls out of stones—but in the final moments of reckoning, nature redefines us. We are born of the earth and to the earth we must one day return. The power and force of life is here all around us, but if we can't balance that energy with love, our life becomes as barren as this dry creek bed."

Ideas to Contemplate

1. Name three ways you can balance the power in your life with love.

2. How does time have dominion over your life?

THE TRUE MEANING OF POWER

When my girlfriend Bonnie learned to drive, her parents always said to her when she drove out the driveway in their small town, "Be sure you don't go past Main Street. Be careful; don't go too far." In the course of my friendship with Bonnie, it became very clear that in every way she had built a fence around her consciousness. For some reason, "Don't go past Main Street" meant "Don't push the envelope of your life experience in any new direction." Bonnie has limited her success, her relationships, and her extraordinary talents because of a past conditioning that she seems incapable of giving up. Don't we all know people around us who do just that despite our love and encouragement? They limit their own power.

Power means many different things to people. It is an invaluable attribute, perhaps one of the most important attributes we can ever explore in our lives. Each of us is related to one another, though we often choose not to see that. *For you to be successful and powerful in your endeavors in your lifetime helps me to become successful and powerful in my lifetime.* Why? Because, if I let you, you inspire me. We are not separate from one another. If we could learn the true anatomy of power, we could solve the environmental problems that are plaguing our planet. We could quell our riots. We could end our wars.

We could also ease our insecurities and our depression. There are currently ten million people in this country alone who are on antidepressant medications. This is a profound statement. It says that we need help. We are living in a more violent society today than ever in history. This is a statement about the misuse of power. It says that we need comfort for our spirit. We need a change and a new point of view. For all of the destruction that we see in our media, on our televisions, in our films, and within our society itself, we need a new concept of what power really is so that we can rebuild what we are currently destroying. *We need to rebuild our ideas about power.*

Power and the energy of life exist within each of us. They give us the ability to feel our own vitality and be able to communicate it to others. Power comes from a sense of focus, well-being, and health, all of which emanate from maintaining a balanced point of view in the world. Power is the energy that flows through all things. Individuals earn access to it by keeping themselves healthy and strong physically, emotionally, and spiritually. We become healthy when we heal the dis-ease in our spirits. The contentment of the soul becomes reflected in our bodies as a glowing state of health and an absence of illness.

I talk a great deal about point of view in my work. I feel that the endeavors in your life—whether these are your acts of power, how you function within your daily work, or how you behave with your family—are all aspects of important communication in your world of power. Your success within your interactions has to do with how you see the world and how you see yourself within the context of your environment. *Defining your self-worth and your intent develops your point of view.*

Imagine a person of power as a wheel, rolling smoothly down the hill, in perfect balance. The wheel doesn't wobble, and there are no warps or holes that throw off the balance. A person of power is whole, with the ability and the strength to see herself through her own eyes rather than through the eyes of another. The wheel of her physicality and her spirit is balanced and in harmony.

Ideas to Contemplate

1. Name three ways that you comfort your soul.

2. Do you have a sense of your point of view in the world? How do you see the world and yourself in the context of your environment?

COMING INTO POWER

In one of my workshops, I worked with a Chinese woman who
had been brought up in a very traditional way. During the work-
shop, many topics arose and many lively discussions took place,
but this woman sat quietly throughout, never uttering a word.
At the end of the day I suggested that my students write a paper
about some of the issues we had touched on and bring it back in
the morning.

When she arrived the next day, the quiet woman shyly
handed me her homework, which was an extraordinarily well-
developed piece of writing, profoundly thought out and expertly
crafted. She obviously had a great gift that needed to be shared
with the rest of us. I challenged her by encouraging her to talk
and express her insights to the group. I knew how difficult this
would be; if speaking to the group proved to be too much for
her, we'd come up with another solution. She fully accepted my
challenge by standing up in front of the room and talking about
her ideas, offering them as a treasured gift. When she had finished speaking and took her seat, her cheeks were flushed and
she was smiling. Everyone felt blessed by her words, but in the
end, she was the one who benefited the most. She had changed
visibly, and we could all see the difference. Most important, she
had changed the way she viewed herself. By taking responsibility for her communications, she had found a way into her
sphere of personal power, something she had denied herself for
a very long time. In giving the gift of love, she had received
power as her reward.

As I wrote in the introduction, power and love must go hand
in hand. They are inexorably linked. One without the other is
like a right side without the left. When love is felt inwardly but
there is an absence of power, the love remains dormant, unable to
reach out and affect the world at large. We feel the love, but we
cannot utilize it as a tool to heal ourselves or to comfort others.

Ideas to Contemplate

1. Is it difficult to express your ideas in front of others? Why or why not?

2. How can you begin to claim the power to express your love in the world? Identify a spiritual, physical, and emotional way.

ACHIEVING HARMONY

Exercising both power and love leads to a balanced and harmonious life—spiritually, physically, emotionally, and mentally. To achieve this balance and harmony in your life, you need an understanding of energy. What is energy? Energy is the whirling protons, electrons, and neutrons that produce friction and heat—I could go on and on—but what creates the movement, the force, the life spirit, but God? Energy is life. Everything is made of energy, including you. Energy is power. If you don't truly understand that you are made of energy, that you are a moving life force that needs direction and intent, then you cannot express who you are in society in a meaningful way.

To have a successful racehorse, you need to feed it well and carefully. If you are an athlete, you need to pay attention to your body: to what you eat, to the appropriate kind of exercise so that you can express yourself in your sport in an optimum way. The same principle holds true for your life as a whole. You need to know everything about the best food for your physical body and the most nourishing food for your spirit so that with all of the energy that you expend in the world, there is something coming back your way, something that nourishes and sustains you, something that makes you feel good and powerful and renewed.

How you express your power helps define your reality. Your use of that power—your intellect, vision, integrity, and intent—defines your relationship with people and the world around you. This book helps you define your power. When you assume power in a conscious way, always balance it with love, if not for a person, then for animals, art, or nature, so that your life becomes more successful, and more harmonious in every respect.

Ideas to Contemplate

1.   When you need love, who or what do you turn to?

2.   Name three ways that love returns to you.

LEARNING FROM FAILURE

To have personal power, it is essential to understand failure and the tendency of all success to regress to the mean average. The true success of your life lies in the effort, the joy you find in optimum efficiency, not in the result. But so often we are owned by the result, seemingly mesmerized by the thoughts of accumulation and recognition and respect. So what's wrong with respect? Nothing. But where does your respect live? If your self-esteem is dependent on the opinion of others, you are destined to fail, because the laws that govern our conscious awareness are fickle and leveling. Without question, animals destroy the weak: Wolves thin out the herds of caribou by identifying the weak members. Humans, on the other hand, destroy those who are unpopular. Why are we so often miserable as a species? Perhaps we would do well to understand that being successful at one thing may mean you have failed completely at something else. You can become a great scientist like Einstein, but the hours of study that it took him may have left huge holes in other parts of his life. Naturally, it is difficult to do everything well, and, more important, it's not necessary! But it is essential to stay aware of where you fail and choose success somewhere else. Understanding your own sort of knowing brings balance through awareness of both your successes and failures.

THE POWER OF KNOWING WHO YOU ARE

There is a great power in knowing who you are. The technique offered below is a useful one that I've often used with people who are trying to gain a clearer understanding of themselves.

In your mind's eye, envision yourself sitting in the center of a circle of stones. Imagine this circle to be like a compass, with north and south, east and west. Allow yourself to ask the question "Who am I?" over and over again. As you ask this question, be aware of your responses as you go deeper and deeper. Knowing who you are and being able to define your essence is one of the most important things you will ever do on your way to personal power. Do this simple exercise often. Self-knowledge has been extolled by all the great philosophies dating back to Socrates and Plato.

For centuries, the ancients have used the circle in various ways to teach the many aspects of personal power. Let's try another. Place four stones in a circle around you or imagine sitting in a beautiful circle of stones in a place like Ireland or Monument Valley in Arizona. Each direction represents part of your being. Close your eyes and center yourself. The south of the circle represents physicalness. As you try to determine who your true self is, first focus on your physical being. How do you express yourself physically in the world? Do you exercise your body through athletics, aerobic routines, or physical work? Do you promote your state of physical health? These would be some of the first questions you would ask. Those who are primarily oriented in the south are very physical people. They love the earth, stones, and crystals. They like the sound of a drum beat. They enjoy work and using their bodies. Do you feel comfortable in your own body?

Now look to the north of your circle of stones. The north represents spirit and the strength and wisdom within your spirit. How do you relate to your god? This is a very important aspect of who you are and how you see and define yourself. How do you open yourself to inspiration and manifest that inspiration into the world? Are you aware of when your energy shifts? Are you open to your sense of power? What is your sense of god? Say a prayer for divine inspiration. Do you have a sense of oneness with all life? A person who is oriented primarily in the northern direction of the circle moves from a position of spiritual strength.

Now look to the west. The western direction of your circle holds your feelings about death, dreams, and transformation. It is where your emotions live. What does transformation mean to you and to your emotional makeup? Do your emotions control you, or do you control your emotions? When? Have you learned to remember your dreams? A person who is oriented primarily in the western part of the circle is best able to manifest dreams into reality. Death is an important aspect of the west. Do you fear death? What do you think happens when you die?

Look to the east of your circle. The eastern direction is the home of mental activity, the meditations of life. How do you think about things? Are you logical? Are you disciplined? Do you approach problems logically? Also living in the eastern direction is the old, wise aspect of self and that part of yourself that tests existing institutions and aspects of life that you consider controlling, such as the government and other political and social structures. Meditate and try to contact the old wise one within you. What does he or she look like? What does he or she have to say to you? Those who are oriented primarily in the eastern part of the circle find it important to question and test their world.

The circle provides an important focusing tool for understanding yourself. As you begin to understand yourself, you
begin to heal yourself, and as you heal yourself, you can then
take your power and heal the world around you. As a society
naturally evolves out of the language that it speaks and therefore
needs to continually create a new vocabulary, so the natural
environment waits for us humans as a species to move creatively
into a new world of enlightened evolution. Have you ever asked
yourself how animals evolve? How does a two-toed horse
become a three-toed horse? By running faster each day than it's
capable of running. We as humans evolve by stretching and
becoming more than we ever dreamed we could be. So *we must
heal our fear of taking our power. The well-being of our world
depends on it.*

CENTERING YOUR POWER

To find and maintain connection with your sense of power,
never leave your center. Count your bad points as well as your
good. What is good and what is bad are most often purely relative. If you sense a weakness within yourself, explore it. It may
become the source of your greatest strength. As you sit like a
sacred Buddha amid the pandemonium of your life, *always
remember that the situation or person who has the ability to upset
you the most, to pull you off center, is your greatest teacher.* Center
yourself in your power, and release your need for constant distraction and your unconscious desire to be led away from who
you really are. One thing I have learned by working with thousands of people over the years is that so often we say we want to
be conscious and free and enlightened, but in reality we are
afraid of our beauty and our power. *We are afraid of becoming
who we are trying to become.* Think about it.

Power means that you have the ability to use your God-given

instruments—your body and mind—to transform what is ordi-
nary into the magnificence of a work of art. Having power
means you act with integrity, complete focus, and clear intent,
whether in writing a book, painting a picture, or detailing a car.
When performed with true power, washing a dish with love can
be as nourishing an experience as buying yourself a diamond
necklace.

Given the extraordinary stress of twentieth-century life, love
and power often seem to be opposing concepts. In truth, they
are not. One is the reflection or shadow of the other, and each
without the other is incomplete. Once we are able to recognize
our personal power and imbue it with love, the glow emanating
from our sense of well-being will automatically illuminate the
environment around us.

Ideas to Contemplate

1. Name three people or situations who pull you off center. Why?

2. Do you recognize who you are—a great, wise being of beauty?

5

Recognizing Love and Claiming Personal Power

What we create in the world,
we must first create within ourselves.
For there to be magic in your life,
you must first believe in magic.

YOUR ACT OF POWER

"If you want power, you have to make a place inside you for power to live," said Agnes as we sat on her porch in the far north. The northern lights illuminated her face with lavender light as she held her fist over her solar plexus, which is her power center.

Over the past decades, many people have asked me how they can better deal with the stresses of twentieth-century life and remain balanced in spirit, balanced in power and love. In turn, I ask them: If you could make one act of power that would change your life forever, what do you think it would be? Oftentimes, this question brings up both unrest and passion, because an act of power is an act that is performed from your strongest passion, out of the depths of your being. If done properly (and there is no other way to do it!), *an act of power is an accurate manifestation of your personal truth in the world around you.*

Many years ago, Agnes Whistling Elk said to me, "*We are all called. We are all chosen. But so very, very few of us have the courage to follow our dreams.*"

For an act of power, you focus all of your desire and all of your energy, and put it into one single endeavor. It's like putting all your eggs in one basket—not a bad idea if, as Mark Twain advised, you "watch that basket"!

An act of power is the visible and artful manifestation of your truth in the world. An act of power is when you take all of your focus, all of your energy, and all of your love, and put it into one endeavor with passion. Look at a sharp knife. The blade is pared away until almost nothing is left. But that tiny edge gets the job done in a way that even a heavy bar of iron couldn't accomplish. Because of its narrowed focus and unhesitating strength, your act of power works like a sword cutting through butter. The use of that edge catapults you up to a place where you and your destiny can begin to mesh.

In fulfilling your act of power, you symbolically move in a vertical south to north direction on the circle you envisioned in the last chapter, taking your ideas and inspiration that come from your god or spirit in the north and manifesting them in the south into your everyday world. In reaping the feedback and the benefits, using the mirror that the act provides to see yourself, you experience newfound wisdom and strength, which you then send back up to the north, the realm of spirit. This vertical movement or act of power pushes through a barrier of energy that has been holding you back your entire life. When you realize that you are afraid to become the balanced and extraordinary

person you're trying to be, then you can release the fears that
hold you back—fear of being powerful and not loved or perhaps
fear of being alone. You move up above the clouds, into the
golden sunlight, into a different level of balance, a different har-
monic, where other people who have made acts of power live.
Even though you have been shoulder to shoulder with these
people of power, perhaps your whole life, you didn't realize that
their lives were so very different from yours.

When you make an act of power, such as writing a book or
expressing your true passion in your life, you begin to manifest
your true destiny in this lifetime. Your true destiny isn't just the
book you write, the masterpiece of art you produce, the magnificent music you create and compose, the family you raise: An
act of power is a gathering of your strength, a gathering of your
energy. This is not dilettantism or a casual decision. It's a burning fire, and in the process of that fire burning, all of your negativity, all of your blocks and emotional baggage, are burned
away. Instead of giving tremendous energy to the problems that
keep you from your act of power, the very fact that you have
made the act of power gets rid of the blocks that you had.

An act of power can only be truly made with an incredible act
of will. *You are born into the physical plane for a reason*—to learn
lessons you can only find on the physical plane, to learn how to
deal with the challenges of life and make your acts of power.
The foundation for your act of power is created by study and
homework about your subject. It must be very strong, just as a
skyscraper cannot be built on sand. When you move into
heightened awareness and begin to do higher spiritual work,
you must be prepared—physically, mentally, and emotionally.
All of your baggage must be left behind if it no longer serves
you.

The act of power requires a tremendous amount of work in
your life. It requires psychological study, physical and spiritual

examination of yourself. Through these mirrors that you have created by working, you have hopefully managed to balance your mind and emotions—the pain, difficulties, and childhood conditioning—and you have gotten closer to the center of your true essence. And you sit in the center of your own circle of truth, in ever-increasing stillness, knowing that you have indeed accomplished what you have come onto this earth to do. You have made your mark. You have added to the world in some way. You have manifested your truth and your beauty, and now a kind of stillness inhabits you. You begin to watch life in all its mystery, like a great wise one who is full of love.

We spend most of our lifetime in reaction to the world around us, to our conditioning, to what people do to us, for us, with us. When you are in touch with your essential reality, you become a prime mover. You begin to be a sacred witness, simply watching, creating harmony and balance and a space of tenderness around you of kindness and understanding.

Ideas to Contemplate

1.   Is your life a process of action or reaction?

2.   Have you learned from your failures?

PREPARING FOR YOUR ACT OF POWER

The principles of gathering and storing are essential in your preparation for your act of power. There are a variety of ways of storing power. For example, learning about focus and educating your abilities to discipline yourself to become impeccable in whatever you choose to do are ways of storing power. Developing your impeccability creates a storehouse within yourself that you can draw upon if need be.

Timing is an integral aspect of personal power. Understanding timing—when to use energy and when not to use it—is crucial. For instance, if you have a big job interview in the near future and the job is all you have ever wanted, you set up your reserves, you prepare, you concentrate, and you hold your power. You school yourself mentally and emotionally, like getting ready for a marathon. You exercise. You don't start off by running a marathon, but you train until you feel ready to run the distance. It's the same way with intent or your sense of will. You store and build and train your power and inner energy until the moment of reckoning.

We are all under tremendous stress in this society. Our lives have changed incredibly. The dollar value for work expended seems to be lessening so that we need more power to attain what would have been much easier a few years ago. It is important to study and observe how much you waste energy, and learn instead how to store energy. We waste energy with negativity in thoughts, such as gossip or addictions to food or abuse. We waste our time in poor organization or laziness. Store energy through exercise, positive thoughts, and spiritual and physical balance. Be active and strong.

When we have gathered power, we are filled with a splendor that is self-generated. We become an expression of radiant energy that illuminates everyone we meet. To fully utilize power, we need to learn techniques for gathering and storing power, as well as coming to terms with timing—when to expend energy and when to hold it.

HOLDING YOUR ENERGY

Picture a place of natural beauty that you love—a mountain, a beach, or anywhere that you can imagine storing your own energy. Imagine pure light moving from your solar plexus and into the mountain. See it glowing. At another time, when you are very depleted, you can go sit with that mountain and regain your energy. See pure light, sensing or visualizing it returning to your navel and filling you with strength and gratefulness. Remember that the success of such an endeavor depends on your will and your intent. Use your will to picture what you want. Your intent actualizes your will and brings what you picture into being. You need to practice and to trust yourself. You can return later with more energy to give back to the mountain. If you were an enlightened being like Jesus or Buddha, that source of energy would always be present. You would be like a piece of hollow bamboo with the wind blowing through it, the wind being energy. But most of us are not perfect beings! We get sidetracked every day. Certain things catch us off guard, surprise us, maybe just biologically, like an illness or a personal conflict. And we fail. We take a wrong step for a moment, maybe for a whole day, and when that happens, we need to have a place where we can go to replenish ourselves. I often go with Agnes Whistling Elk to Skeleton Canyon in the Superstition Mountains of southern Arizona. I sit beneath the jagged peaks at sunset, watching the pink and orange glow bring the ancient stone to life. The west wind is my friend, and as I call to it, it caresses me with renewed strength and love.

So go to your mountain. Or maybe it's a beautiful tree or a park with a particular bench you love to sit on. Maybe you can actually plant a tree. Get to know your tree. Give it energy, and it in turn will give energy back to you. But you have to know how to do this. Sit with love and an open heart. A good relationship with the tree's spirit and life force is all that's required. It's like having a big battery. Whether it's a tree, a mountain, or a big rock you go to, you can make it sacred by honoring its existence with your light and your care. You can have a dialogue with that energy form. You can even store energy in a regular old car bat-

tery, but this doesn't work so well for me, because to me an old
car battery isn't beautiful! I need something of beauty to inspire
me in terms of storing power. Beauty is truth, so if something
beautiful teaches me, great. I can have an exchange with it. And
if I need energy, I can take it and bring it back.

Native peoples have practiced this art for millennia. Every
tribe, every nation has its medicine people, and the mountains
and all living things on this earth have been sources of energy
and power for those nations throughout history. But you need to
look around you in your immediate environment and find the
places of power close to you. These are simple places that will
call to you by making you feel more peaceful or stronger. The air
temperature may change as you approach. These places are
there, even if you can't think of a location at the moment. You
can find them and make them places of power for you with your
recognition and energy. *To have a relationship with power, you
have to sit with power. You have to give it your time. Power tests
you always.* It is a whole relationship with energy forces. Begin
now to listen. Be aware of power sitting next to you—waiting
and wanting to be heard.

Years ago I had been searching for a power place near my
home in Los Angeles. Frustrated, I went out into my garden and
sat under my lemon tree, where I often sat because I felt medita-
tive and calm there. Agnes sat on a rock nearby, smiling like a
laughing Buddha. Presently a hummingbird came up to my nose
whirring its wings and then flew around my head several times
before flying away.

"Well, Little Wolf, have you found your power place yet, or
does the Hollywood sign on the mountain have to fall on your
head to get your attention?" Agnes asked me.

"Okay," I said laughing, "but I thought something earth-
shaking would happen."

"A power place brings a sense of well-being and personal ceremony—a ceremony of introspection and positive action at the same time. A place of power brings you closer to the divine," the old Indian woman said, her eyes shining like mirrors as she sat serenely in the shadows of the garden.

That lemon tree has become a longtime friend and source of power for me, as has the hummingbird, which is a symbol to me of great courage and endurance. You, too, if you look, may find a place of power closer to home than you expected.

Ideas to Contemplate

1. Have you ever found a place of power? How did you honor that place?

2. Where is the place of power in your home—the area where you feel most peaceful and confident?

3. What natural setting makes you feel most empowered—the mountains, ocean, desert, trees, rocks—and why?

6

The Soul of Power

Everything you need is here. The things you need are always here; you need to be smart enough to find them.

We are moving into a new millennium, and to transit through this extraordinary gateway we truly need to let go of that which no longer serves us. More important, we need new tools and a new way of living to learn from, and successfully face, the challenges that are before us. When facing a particularly difficult challenge, it is important to move whatever obstacles need to be moved, to step into your power and create your own reality. It is possible to move mountains when your intent declares it so.

Containing your power so that it can be used at will is a fine art. Allowing someone to drain that power is self-defeating. I'll help you learn to discern between those who support you in being a powerful person and those who drain you of your vitality. Just as a camel stores water for later use, we can practice focusing our attention in such a way that we become a veritable storehouse of energy.

When power is expressed outwardly in the absence of an open heart, it becomes the aggressive embodiment of dominance and ego. It drains energy rather than providing nourishment. I had a personal experience of this during one of the horse competitions I was participating in. I had a particular trainer whom I loved dearly and who loved me. We had worked together since I was a small child, but he inadvertently gave me the unfortunate experience of draining my power.

It was ten minutes before a national event. I was working in the practice arena just before my scheduled time to ride when this trainer came at me quite aggressively. He kept barking a particular command, but I could not understand what he was asking of me. If he had slowed down, opened his heart, and spoken gently to me, I would have been able to hear him. But between his frustration that I wasn't getting the message and the high tension brought on by the competition, somehow he wasn't able to communicate properly. He finally began yelling at me at the top of his lungs.

I had worked with this man for many years and loved him very much. I was so vulnerable and open to him that his angry words affected me profoundly. I burst into tears. As I entered the arena, I could feel the confidence draining from my cells like water running from an open tap. Needless to say, this was not my best competition and I was eliminated quickly. My trainer and I both learned a good lesson: Anger and abuse can drain the power right out of you. All the work I had done, all my practice and defining of power in the weeks leading up to this competition, were undone in one moment of anger and frustration.

SURRENDERING TO DIVINE SPIRIT

While my trainer drained my energy unintentionally, you will also encounter people in life who do not wish you well. The more you glow, the more they will try to take away your glow and hinder your progress. Some will even take pleasure in your failures. But you can guard against such attacks and can protect yourself from people who might try to drain your energy.

When others hurt you, a piece of your spirit goes out to them. This is known as giving away your power. When my trainer hurt me, I became fragmented and "lesser." That night I lay down and meditated. I imaged the situation all over again. I felt my pain, and then I redesigned the event. I saw a little piece of my spirit all mangled, the piece that had been left with him. I plumped it up, healed it, and called it back inside of me. *You have an honored partnership with your spirit.* I had let myself down by splitting off, becoming weak, and listening to abuse. I had broken my sacred agreement with my spirit by letting go of responsibility for my health and my balance. But I healed the situation and learned something, just as you can. When you're hurt, meditate, re-create the event, bring your spirit back, and heal yourself. Know that your hurtful situation has been transformed. "Believe as if it were true now" is a powerful affirmation from the Book of David. Use this idea and bring yourself back into the present.

Your awareness can guide you like the rudder on a boat, keeping you from floundering and wandering into box canyons where no amount of energy can extricate you. Sensitivity and awareness are like antennae that pick up the misuse of power by individuals who cross your path. Understanding these experiences can teach you to use the intelligence that lives within your own body so that, without harm, you can move forward and around obstacles the way a river flows around rocks. And with each move, as you witness how others use negativity, you gain power through the friction of energy that is created. You learn about the ebb and flow of energy and sensitivity. You feel it and flow with it. You rest at the proper times. You may even move at times into a state of invisibility where you sit quietly in a place of stillness and silence, gathering power for the next flow, for the next time it is appropriate.

Sensitivity and awareness are your building blocks to power. If you are sensitive to the world around you, then you do not take unconsciously from the pool of life force without giving back energy in a like kind for what you have received. When you sit down to eat, acknowledge the life form that has given so that you may live. To take energy unconsciously is to not give back, is to think that you own this energy without any thought for the other life forms around you. Be sensitive to the process of awareness. Wake up to your senses and feel the coolness of a breeze on your skin like silk. Be aware of other people's needs as well as your own. Out of ignorance we add to another's pain without thinking. *Be aware of the magnificent instrument that your body is, a gift from the spiritual radiance that surrounds you.* This all comes with sensitivity and awareness and leads you to power. But for you to share that power, you must first have love—love for your own abilities and for all aspects of life. In this way, you become a part of the perfect balance in nature.

Years ago, I left what many friends called an idyllic life because I felt a great yearning for the wilderness and the balance and harmony I found there. I began to learn about awareness and higher consciousness from a great woman who lived there. Her native friends call her "The One Who Knows How." By listening to the winds walking in the mountains, I began to hear the silence within me and to learn to love myself. I had never stopped long enough to hear the great teacher that lives within me. With education, and by giving up what no longer served me and moving into the center of my fears, I began to nurture all aspects of myself for the first time. I learned what it meant to surrender myself unconditionally to divine spirit.

ANIMALS OF POWER

All people have verbal and nonverbal ways of communicating, which let others know what energies they contain. We communicate through body language, through words, and through symbolic acts of creation. In ancient times, and oftentimes still today, Native Americans carried shields or placed shields on tripods in front of their lodges. These shields were painted with symbols that defined the owner's spiritual background. The images depicted the work the person had accomplished not only in the physical world but in the world of spirit. Frequently the images included power animals. Warriors would spend years in preparation for the sacred time when they would journey alone to a mountaintop or sacred ground to seek a vision. Their conversation with the Great Spirit would illuminate the direction of their path. Included in this quest was the search for an animal of power that would lend strength and wisdom to their life. This animal or bird would present itself to them, and its energy and power, if honored properly, would stay with them for life.

Nonnative people also have their power animals, but for the most part are unaware of them. We have our instincts and our original nature that yearns to be expressed, but we don't know how. There is a wildness in all of us that loves the earth and wants to speak and to be heard. We repress the perfection of that nature and rarely allow ourselves to do ceremony or experience the wildness of our own souls. We forget to communicate our feelings and instincts through dance, singing, dreaming, or performance as people have done throughout history. We have lost touch, it seems, with the more spontaneous aspect of ourselves. So we hide who we truly are because our culture no longer values living in an instinctual, intuitive way.

Often I take people on a ceremonial journey where they meet their power animal. This frequently changes their lives. A woman told me after this experience not long ago that the whole idea had fascinated her, but she couldn't see how this related to her life as a health-care worker. What she discovered was that her animal was a cougar. I explained to her that a cougar is a very predatory animal. She asked me if people were nervous around her because of her power animal.

"Yes," I told her. "If you are predatory, your eyes are very strong, and people who are less predatory will become nervous and fidgety under your gaze if you are not careful." I explained that she needed to soften her eyes and her body language so that people would not react to her in that way. We sense power animals in people in very subtle ways. This woman became much more successful in her work after reaching this under-standing. To understand your power animal puts you in touch with the harmony of Mother Earth and the true nature of things.

I often think about animals of power when I think about peo-ple I know. When I am working with people, I will notice that their attitudes and body language mimic some animal of power. One woman who is a very good friend contains her energy in an interesting way. When she sits before me, she resembles a cheetah, the fastest sprinter in the animal kingdom. Like a cheetah, she sits very still, with tremendous presence and self-containment, as if she totally understands her power in the world. She sits without movement, poised, until the proper moment arises. When she draws on her energy, she is much like a feline drawing on its power. She moves out into the world fast, wasting no energy. In a sense, she moves directly toward her prey, whether that is an idea, a colleague, or a new account. She is very predatory in her view of the world, but not in a neg-ative way. She knows what she wants, and she goes for it when appropriate.

Getting a sense of your power animal can help you identify what you are truly about. A power animal is part of you and helps you build power and focus energy. We need to relearn how to know ourselves in this way. If you are a bear, no wonder you rest in the winter and don't like to start new projects until spring. Knowing your power animal means knowing yourself better. How can you define who you actually are if you do not really and truly have the experience of knowing who you are on an instinctual level?

MANIFESTING YOUR DREAMS

Some people have told me that even though they have taken their power in their lives, even though they've performed their acts of power, they are still unhappy. Like John and Laura, who are world-renowned literary agents and happily married, they have moments of joy, moments of happiness, but for the most part their lives are filled with stress and confusion and a kind of emptiness. When I consider what power really means—manifesting your dreams, manifesting your true self in the world— I've come to realize that most people don't know the essence of who they really are. So many of us live through a kind of suspended self, rather than a genuine self. John and Laura are very successful and they love each other, but they have no sense of spirit or love for something greater than themselves. Is that important? I think so, because God is love, and I don't know how you can experience a true feeling of love without a love for all creation, which, for me, encompasses some concept of a god.

Power is a manifestation of whatever you divine as your need, your desire, your essence in the world. If there is not love at the base of that power, then power is a container that is often filled with emptiness. Love has been described by the author and therapist R. D. Laing as disguised violence. In the 1960s, we all talked about love as the answer to everything. But what is love? *True love is a different kind of emptiness. It is a stillness within your spirit that creates a vacuum, an opening, into which the bliss of God can enter.* At that moment, you become truly aware. You become aware of nature, and your relationships to the spirit of life that surrounds you. You become aware of your place within the scheme of things.

We are called upon to hold within us the truth that we are all part of a oneness. This oneness is not a static state, but a movement of power through the abyss of chaos and striving into the world of compassion and understanding and love. Without love, in a sense, there is no life. Love can be manifested in many ways. It can be love for another person—and what a beautiful, wonderful gift that is—but the most important thing of all is the love of self. The love of self and spirit is the most magnificent realization that can be. You are made of love, because God is love, and you are God in the sense that you are a reflection of the creation of all that is. *All the answers, all the questions that have ever been asked, are within your own being.* But so often we don't know how to access the great bank of knowledge and wisdom that we hold within.

So how do we find it? We find it by tearing away the veils of ignorance and illusion and by moving deeper into the still point of true self. You begin to access this knowledge by examining the mirrors that you have created for yourself. Your job, whether you're a housewife or a lawyer, is a mirror you built to learn from. It reflects your strengths and weaknesses. Are you as organized and disciplined as you thought? Are you a leader or would you rather help someone else be the star? How about your close relationships? Can you accept being loved? Do you need to be in control? Look deeply and honestly into your mirrors and ask questions of yourself. This is a spiritual experience, but it is not a belief structure. There is a huge difference. You do not have to believe in anything but the power and the creativity and the harmony of your own nature. You can't see life through someone else's eyes, you can't live someone else's dream, and be happy.

The bridge between the physical and the spiritual is created by an act of power that can only be made by you, that can only be made from your heart. That act of power is an act of gratefulness. You can be aware of everything. You can make your acts of power. You can become a millionaire many times over as you receive the abundance of this universe, and you can do it consciously. But still, you may be bereft of the understanding of love. Without love, what is power anyway? You can have all the money in the world, you can have all the position and the power; but without love, life is empty. *Without love, there is no fulfillment, because without love we cannot know God.* And that is the human tragedy.

In their ignorance, many people try to fill their emptiness with belief structures. We try to gather belief structures around us and say, "Well, I believe in God," but without the experience of God. And if we don't experience God, we don't experience love, and there is no opening in our hearts.

If you could sit for a moment, simply sit in meditation and create a small ritual for yourself, a ritual of sacredness, of respect, and think about all of the things in your life that you are grateful for, you could begin to move beyond this impasse. You could begin to contain both power and love. There is always something you are grateful for. You have the opportunity to be reading this work and to be trying to evolve toward a place of self-realization. Be grateful for that. Be grateful for your health, for the opportunity to create mirrors in this lifetime that can enlighten you. All the choices you make in life, such as partners, jobs, hobbies, and games, are mirrors that you create to learn from. Open your heart to contain all of who you are, all of what life truly is; this is the path of mastery.

Ideas to Contemplate

1. Do you know when it is important to rest and hold your power? How do you rest?

2. Have you ever sensed a power animal near you? Describe what it was like.

3. What animal would you be if you could choose?

Duality: Realizing the Wonder

PART III

As once the winged energy of delight
carried you over childhood's dark abysses,
now beyond your own life build the great
arch of unimagined bridges.
Wonders happen if we can succeed
in passing through the harshest danger;
but only in a bright and purely granted
achievement can we realize the wonder.
To work with Things in the indescribable
relationship is not too hard for us;
the pattern grows more intricate and subtle,
and being swept along is not enough.
Take your practiced powers and stretch them out
until they span the chasm between two
contradictions . . . For the god
wants to know himself in you.

—RAINER MARIA RILKE

7

Finding a Worthy Opponent

Duality is what makes us feel alone.
We as humans separate ourselves, and that is our tragedy.

I sometimes liken the ferocious pace of our lives to the energy of a cyclone. We try to hold our ground in the middle of it, searching for a way to stay in balance while the storm swirls around us. The winds of change blow constantly, alternately bringing us tremendous danger and extraordinary beauty. The dual nature of all things—love and hate, health and disease, balance and chaos—expresses itself in this metaphor of standing firm in the center of the cyclone. When you can maintain your balance in the ever-shifting duality of life, you are choosing to live in a masterful way.

Being blindly trapped by duality keeps us from mastery. *Duality is what makes us feel alone.* It keeps us apart from all other living things. It keeps us from being in true harmony with the earth because we so often do not feel part of nature. *We as humans separate ourselves, and that is our tragedy.* But duality is a reality of physical existence. In working with how we react to and feel about the sense of separation or duality we have created, our task is not to integrate two seemingly disparate aspects. We cannot merge a man with a woman, for example, and expect to find some sort of androgynous being who is whole and complete. Rather, the task is to divine a new vantage point or perspective in which we can allow two opposite forces to live in harmony. This is mastering the idea of duality, which allows us to take the next step along our path to enlightenment.

THE PARADOX OF POWER

An old wise woman taught me the first and last lesson of power. The first lesson is that we are all alone. The last is that we are all one.

Although these ideas appear to be diametrically opposed, in truth they are not. As this woman and I sat at the edge of a precipice, our feet dangling high above a seemingly endless abyss, she pointed to the other side of the great canyon that stretched out before us. "Symbolically," she said, "we stand on opposite sides of this chasm. I stand on one side in peace and freedom, because I know that we are all one. You sit on the other side trapped by a millstone around your neck. That millstone is created by your self-imposed fears. You think you are alone.

"*As you see, we sit together, both all one and all alone. Such is the illusion of life.* You must create a bridge from one side of the chasm to the other through your faith and trust, believing that your dreams can be realized. When you drop your fears into the abyss, only then can you merge the seeming duality of life. Then you will become a master."

There is a great opportunity for experience and growth

between the two concepts that old wise woman shared with me. The first lesson of power—that we are all alone—is important to understand fully. Stand within your aloneness and your emptiness so that you absolutely and totally own the idea and the experience. I'll give you an example. Sally, a young woman I was working with, began a new job. She had been preparing for this job for several years. After the first two weeks, she came to see me. She knew no one in the company, and she felt like an outsider, very alone.

"I don't know if I can go on, Lynn. Everyone is so cold to me. I feel so isolated."

"This is a great opportunity, Sally, for you to fully experience and claim the first lesson of power," I said, smiling at her.

"I don't understand."

"You must first own your aloneness before you can give it up. To stand alone in the center of your abilities and your integrity is very hard to do. But this is your chance to feel how strong you really are. Then you can go on to integrate your strength with the abilities of those around you."

We talked for a while, and Sally recentered herself. She saw her job differently and approached the social aspect of it from a new perspective. A month later, Sally returned and told me she had learned a great lesson. "I allowed myself to feel completely separate, different, and alone. I owned that feeling and didn't fight it. I understand something new about surrender. So now what?" she asked.

"Now you can cross that great abyss. At the other side, you will find a new and beautiful experience. You will discover that we are all one. You will feel the oneness of all life. But you had to fully experience your separateness first."

This brings me back to the subject of duality. In this physical existence called life experience, we see the result of duality every day; when we see war, when we see disease, when we see gang riots and killings, we are seeing the effects of duality.

War comes from the idea and the belief that I am here and you are there, and we are separate. There is a great weakness in this concept. In blindly accepting the concept of duality, you will always lose, because you become lost in a deadly game of social power. The game of social power is very different from the game of personal power. In personal power, you honor a worthy opponent, which I'll explain later. In the game of social power, you are trying to win over someone else. That immediately puts you in a one-down position, which is an aggressive, confrontational position of separation. If you are trying to live in true power, this one-down position will defeat you at every turn. You are caught before a vast chasm of duality where you are forever distanced from others whom you wish to dominate.

The first step toward bridging the chasm of duality is accepting life as it is. When you understand that complete acceptance of yourself will open your heart, increase your power, and thereby offer you the opportunity to be whole, you will no longer view yourself as separate. In the light of your acceptance, duality disappears, and you become fully committed to love, which really means that you fully love who you are and what you stand for in life. *Remember that love is power.*

As you choose a different point of view, a point of view centered in personal power yet beyond duality, you will then experience a very different feeling and a very different sense of success. You will experience a sense of oneness with everything around you.

One afternoon, while I was in Nepal with Ani, a Nepalese hill woman and teacher of mine, she pointed up to Anapurna in the Himalaya mountain range and said to me, "We're like that mountain, partially hidden by clouds. The extent of her power and beauty is hidden from view; at the top she is lost in a dream. Before we are born onto this earth walk, we wait for a great blessing—our chance to be born onto earth. We know that we come here to be enlightened. When we are born, the dream begins. Like the cloud hiding the mountaintop, the concept of separation obscures our true vision. We must gather a strong wind of wisdom to blow away the clouds. Then we can see, truly see, the whole of our being—the silent mountain that we are. That is what life is all about: waking up from the dream. We have come here to be enlightened, yet it is the one thing we are most afraid of."

When you experience oneness, you make a place within yourself for the essence of power, the force of power, to live. You become an invincible warrior in the world, because there is no vulnerable spot for anything to enter to take your power. Energy-draining thoughts, comments, and individuals can only circle you, looking for a hole, looking for a place of sensitivity and weakness, but never finding one.

A sense of oneness with all living things brings with it a sense of personal power. If you come upon a challenge, you honor it as a worthy opponent if you have personal power. Agnes Whistling Elk explained this to me in a wonderful way. We were sitting on her cabin porch in northern Manitoba, Canada, watching the play of the aurora borealis across the sky in crimson and green pulsating sheets of radiant light.

"In the old way," Agnes said, "when a warrior from another nation came into camp, we always gave him the best lodge to sleep in, the choicest food to eat, and the fastest pony to ride. When a warrior was challenged by another, and they both had personal power, they each wanted the other to be the best he could be."

"But why?" I asked.

"Because the stronger your opponent is, the better you have to be. You become more than you ever dreamed you could be. That's how you grow. You don't hate someone who is better than you. You learn from them and eventually overtake them with honor. It's a different way of looking. It is not competition. That's the way it has always been," she said.

"If you have a point of view that takes in the entirety of the living universe, then you live in the center of the world circle of power, as do all others who see the world in this way. This is the essence of personal power—the last lesson of power is that we are all one." Agnes smiled at me and gently pinched my arm.

Ideas to Contemplate

1.   Do I feel separate from others? Why?

2.   How do I accept people who are from a different belief system or culture than my own?

3.   Describe three effects that competition has on you (for example: I'm not worthy; I don't deserve to win; or I feel powerful).

4.   When I'm confronted with a challenge in my relationships or at work, do I accept myself as I am or do I try to become someone who I am not?

8

Good Versus Evil and the Sacred Dream

We must know and embrace all of what we are.
Whatever we choose not to look at will end up ruling our lives.

INTEGRATING BODY AND SOUL

In the process of integrating body and soul, of embracing the truth that all is one, do we really integrate everything, even that which seems disparate, or do we simply find a new vantage point, a new perspective, from which to observe our differences? Let's take, for instance, the concept of good and evil. Oftentimes we think that aspects of the soul—for example, our relationship with ideals or with God—are good, but aspects like desire or money are related to the body and are therefore bad.

A possible new vantage point between good and evil is the understanding that *we cannot disown parts of ourselves or separate body from soul and then expect to find wholeness.* I think I can say that unwittingly we do a kind of evil to ourselves if we have lived through traumas or abuse in life. The impact of trauma creates the loss of soul—pieces of your own soul that are left behind at the event. The result is loss of power and often much more. For many people, it is hard to accept that the retrieval of soul is possible or even actually happens. Let me tell you about an experience I had that made a believer out of me.

In the first year of working with Agnes Whistling Elk and Ruby Plenty Chiefs, my elder women teachers in northern Canada, I shared an extraordinary event with them. July was a young girl who had been learning from Ruby for several years. She was bright, beautiful, and extremely talented in the healing arts. One morning I awoke in Agnes's cabin to the plaintive sounds of flute music outside on the porch. Agnes was gone. I threw on some clothes and slowly opened the cabin door. There sitting on the porch was July playing discordant notes on her flute.

"Good morning, July," I said, sitting next to her. Tendrils of ground fog were encircling the cabin and floating on the early morning air currents rising from the creek below. She didn't answer me, and her eyes were strangely glazed and staring. I touched her shoulder, suddenly very alarmed. She simply kept on playing the flute.

"She has lost part of her soul." Ruby's voice startled me from behind. I swiveled my head around to her find her standing above me, hands on hips and furious.

"What's happened?" I asked.

"She was abused last night by Red Dog," she said. "We will do ceremony and find the piece of her soul that has flown away. Then I will deal with that evil man. He must be stopped."

That night I witnessed and lent my energy to a soul retrieval ceremony. What Ruby meant by saying that July's soul had flown away was that the trauma of physical abuse had broken her spirit and a piece of her soul had left. The result was that July was almost catatonic. July could have been any abused girl on the streets of New York or Los Angeles. Had we not done the ceremony, where Ruby traveled out into the dimensions of dreaming and found and returned her broken soul, then she might possibly have been hospitalized as a mental patient. As it was, July was visibly affected by Ruby's journey, and by morning she was her normal, albeit exhausted, self. I saw it happen myself. Ruby had been trained most of her life to perform what seemed like a miracle to me. I have heard doctors and metaphysicians and ministers explain this phenomenon in many energetic ways.

Even though soul retrieval may sound incredibly unbelievable and far out, the issue really is not whether you believe in this or not. Rather, the point is that when you separate body and soul, you do create an illness of the mind and emotions. *We must know and embrace all of what we are.*

In every one of us lies a magnificent goodness, that part of us which is God, and also a dark shadow self. This is our instinctual nature, the wild part of all of us that may not be so readily accepted within the confines of societal values. Still, our instinctual nature cannot be denied without cutting ourselves off from our power.

We cannot banish that which we consider unacceptable by avoiding it. *Whatever we choose* not *to look at will end up ruling our lives.* That which is unexplored within us festers, gaining tremendous energy, with the potential to become evil. Conversely, that which is well explored opens further and further with the potential of bringing us closer to God. It is important to remember that exploring the shadow will one day bring the shadow itself into the light. *Exploring your instincts and your native creativity integrates your body with your soul.*

Most people fear venturing into the unknown. We are afraid that as we look at evil, it will look back at us, seducing us into its dark world. In fact, it does look back at us, but we need not be drawn to it. Most of us are afraid to move into the unknown, uncharted parts of our being. But when we take the challenge and move into those parts of ourselves that we have never before explored, we may see evil aspects, like our desire to control the lives of others or to manipulate them or events for our own gain. Evil has a power of its own, and a fascination. As you begin to dance with evil to understand it, sometimes that dance seems to have a life of its own that begins to seduce you into a world that does not serve you.

You move out of evil by remembering who you are, by remembering the divine part of your nature. To become completely aligned with the forces of goodness in your life, it is important to move into a state of grace. When you demonstrate the courage to look at all aspects of yourself, you will gain the strength to move away from possible evil into gratefulness. You'll feel grateful for the magnificent life you have been graced with, grateful for the experience of the forces of nature that surround you, grateful for the consciousness and the awareness to experience spirit in your life.

A dear friend of mine, Sin Corazon from southern Mexico, was on a path to enlightenment, but she had always been fascinated by the evil side of magic. So she fell away from our friendship into the study of the dark arts. For years she was lost to me and to herself. Then she met Julio and fell deeply in love. It was their love that finally saved and transformed Sin Corazon into the great *curandera,* or healer, that she is today. This is a state of grace, the heartbeat of God and the Goddess. When we meet the challenge of exploring our own depths, we will be rewarded with even more light.

EVIL MEANS MISSING THE MARK

Power often has to do with the understanding of good and evil and what that means in your own life. For example, dark souls never kill people directly. They make you destroy yourself by capitalizing on your fears. You become so terrified that you create the feared event and bring it into being.

Ideas to Contemplate

1. Do you know anyone who manipulates you?

2. Do you try to control others?

3. Do you have fear around this subject?

4. How can there be fear if all things are created by God?

This book does not discuss the use of power within acts of evil, because to me acts of power are by definition acts of goodness and right-mindedness. Acts of power having to do with evil and darkness are in reality acts of manipulation, energy forms produced through envy and greed. Those people who are not driven by envy and greed cannot commit acts of evil. They will not choose to exercise themselves in that arena. The exercise of personal power is never a manipulation.

Once power is expressed as a manipulation, it becomes a part of darkness. True power has to do with life force. It has to do with making your mark in the world. The hieroglyph for evil in ancient Egypt is rendered as a target, which, translated, means evil when one misses the mark. True power has to do with hitting the center of your chosen target, whether it be a relationship, a job, a spiritual insight—finding the space within you that expresses your personal best. Somehow personal power aug-

ments the reality that already exists. It never detracts; it illuminates. Hitting the mark has to do with defining your target carefully and with integrity.

A FRIEND'S DILEMMA

While some of my concerns about evil do indeed point to the
shadow side of ourselves or our culture that are manifested into
acts that injure or harm others, some of my concerns simply
stem from our misunderstanding of the true nature of energy
and the inherent goodness of the universe. I am reminded of a
chance spring encounter with my friend Janet.

The tall cottonwood trees standing like sentinels along the
Acequia Madre in downtown Santa Fe, New Mexico, began to
stir. Their spring leaves quaked in the first glow of morning
light. I knelt by the slowly moving water, which is so sacred to
the landowners there, and held the palm of my hand over the
tiny reflections of sunlight, pure and radiant, rippling on its surface. Simple, I thought, and yet powerful, how this water brings
life and sustains the Spirits of Place. "Goethe's final words:
'More light,'" a familiar voice said from behind me.

"Good morning, Janet." I hugged my old friend. "You're up
early."

"I haven't been sleeping well," Janet said, with a look of dejec-
tion. "Can we walk?" she asked.

"Sure. I was on my way to Jerry's, my favorite breakfast spot.
Join me."

"If you're buying."

"Of course," I said, looking at her with curiosity. "Is something wrong?" I asked of my friend.

"I'm losing my studio."

"What! You've been there for years."

"Can't afford it. I just can't sell my new paintings. They're beautiful. I don't understand why they're not selling!" Tears welled up in her big brown eyes.

We sat down, lucky to get a seat even at dawn, and ordered French toast and eggs. I watched Janet over sips of tea from a heavy porcelain mug. Her eyes darted around; she was clearly uncomfortable, and her demeanor was completely unlike her.

"This isn't about art, Janet. I really don't think so. I've seen your paintings, and they're inspiring. The colors are vibrant and should appeal to most."

"Then what, Lynn? Look, we're friends, but you see into things. Please help me; talk to me." Janet reached into her pocket and held out her favorite crystal. I took it carefully. I held it to my heart for a moment.

"Well, I do see something, and I would love to share it with you, dear friend, but I may go on for a while, so hear me out, okay?" Janet nodded with a hint of a smile as she dug into her French toast.

"Janet, let's talk about money. Money is a sacred tool. I'm sure that you are sitting here going, 'Humph, money can't be a sacred tool.' But do you feel like that?" I asked, not waiting for an answer. "How about the love of money? Have you the awareness that the universe is abundant and that all things are made by the Great Spirit or God, including money?"

"Well, no. I don't usually like people with money," she said.

"Money is simply the trade beads of the twentieth century, Janet," I went on, "but we have this strange ethic that tells us that money is the root of all evil. But the real root of all evil is using money without consciousness. Simply that. Money is a great tool when it provides freedom. And freedom is what you need—freedom to find your consciousness, to find the goodness in life, to paint and be able to share your painting with others, to be able to educate through the beauty of your art.

"I'd like to ask you a question, Janet. Do you believe in God or a creator?"

"Yes."

"Think about humbleness, a feeling which comes from the understanding that all things great or small are equally powerful and important. Once when I was with my teacher, Agnes Whistling Elk, she handed me a turkey feather. She said to me, 'Here, Lynn, is an eagle feather for you.' And I said, 'Agnes, that's not an eagle feather. That's a turkey feather.' We went round and round about that. The teaching here is that all feathers are eagle feathers, in a way. Even though the eagle has a special ability and power, all things are still the reflections of the Great Spirit. So humbleness lies at the heart of this wisdom.

"Then there is your trust in the sacred dream of life. You must trust that the talents that you have been given are real and true. You must trust that what was given to you was given from the Great Spirit, and when you return your gift of talent by creating meaningful works of art, the Great Spirit will welcome it with open arms. It is part of the exchange. It is part of the give and take of nature, and of the harmony and balance of all that lives. You implode energy, and you explode energy. It's the sacred dance, the movement of life. If that implosion stops and there is only explosion, you move into stasis and the beginning of death. If there is only implosion, thoughts of beauty and no creation of art, no explosion, again you begin to find stasis and the beginnings of death. Life is the process of movement. *And enlightenment is found in the movement between inspiration and the manifestation of that inspiration.* Bringing spirit into your physical life and manifesting your intuitions from spirit creates your art, money, movement, and success.

"Janet, do you feel grateful for your beauty and your art?" I asked, sipping more tea.

"I guess so. But sometimes I feel my need to paint is a curse."

"Then you have a problem. There is no sacred give-away or exchange for the gift you've received. In giving back to God, be grateful that spirit is with you, Janet. If you will express this gratefulness so that your heart expands, you have a direct communication with your creator in the process."

"But why gratefulness?" Janet asked, eating the last piece of French toast.

"Because gratefulness is an act that opens your heart and connects you with your creativity. The forces of life must provide an exchange of energy for that life to continue," I said. "You have received much, so what about giving back?"

"But I have no money!"

"What about beauty, love, spirit?" I asked. "And discernment. Think about what you are giving away. Think about the process of life, the cycles of life, the implosions of energy and the explosions of energy. You discern the best you can give away. Create a painting that pushes the envelope of your entire being. What would please the Great Spirit? What would please you? In this instance of giving away, what you give and what you get have to be equal. You have to give from the heart with no clinging. Clinging would be like saying, 'I'd give it to you, but I'd rather keep it for myself.' You must give away openly and completely. You have much to give, Janet, but you are only thinking about what's coming in!"

"No, I'm not!" Janet said indignantly.

"Yes, you are," I said. "When you are sitting in the center of your power, you are conjuring the position of your self with God, with the Great Spirit. You are considering where you live in the heart of the Great Spirit, and where the Great Spirit lives in the heart of you," I said, and we considered each other for a long time.

"I think in my life today this is the thing I forget: That the Great Spirit is within me, and the Great Spirit is good. I am the Great Spirit, and the Great Spirit is me. I forget that," Janet said, tears filling her eyes.

"Janet, was there an event in your childhood that influenced your relationship to money? Think about it. It's something to really contemplate. I think a lot of people who have poverty consciousness or who sabotage their success developed this attitude in childhood, when somehow it wasn't okay to be someone who was successful, someone who had money," I said, placing my hand gently over hers.

"I never thought about it that way. Yes, my father and mother both thought all successful people were evil," Janet said, tears rolling down her cheeks.

"So let's change how you feel about this," I said. "Are you emotionally prepared to accept money?"

"I'll work on it," Janet said.

"Do you have a place inside you for money to live? Over and over again, people talk to me about not having enough money. But there's no place in them for money to live because they don't like it. Why would money come into you, Janet, if you don't really like it? If you think it's evil, or an end in itself, it's going to fly away. If you love money, if you love what it gives you, if you love money as a means of exchange, money in a sense replies, 'I'm appreciated,' and you've done a good job; you've done well. Bravo. That's great. There is nothing wrong with that, and abundance comes in. That's not like worshiping money as an end in itself. It's seeing money as another form of energy. Light a candle for that," I suggested.

"But I feel all tight and fearful around the subject of success and money," Janet said.

"Physical constraint around taking your deserved success is a tightness in you. You get all tight. You get a little quarter and you won't share it with anyone because you think you won't get another quarter. One of your lessons in life is to learn about money. Do not make it your god, but be open to accepting the gifts of spirit. Money is a gift of spirit. Money is how we trade in this society. So it's important for you to have a relationship with spirit that allows for this exchange," I said, giving Janet a tissue.

"If you don't establish this relationship, you're not going to have any money, and your muses and your art will suffer terribly, to say nothing about your health. And that's ridiculous! In a universe that is so abundant, you should not be without money. If you are without money, then you know that you have something to learn."

"But what about the sacredness of art and my spirit?" Janet wailed as if she hadn't heard a word I had said.

"This is a spiritual lesson. It's not about money. It's about you and how you stop the energy flow from going through your body. That reservation will keep people from buying your paintings. If you stop that energy flow with something as obvious as money, then you're going to produce disease out of the dis-ease about your feelings. *Stopping your own abundance and flow creates energy knots in your body*. Your constraint around the whole subject leaves your art, your great gifts, waiting and alone, just like you—and all for nothing," I said.

As I left my friend to ponder these ideas, I was struck again with the ways we all get off track, the ways we misunderstand the true nature of energy. Often we fear our own power and we don't trust the love that will keep it balanced and in alignment with the ultimate good of all.

Ideas to Contemplate

1.   How do I feel about money?

2.   Where do I feel stuck in my body? In my life?

3.   What is my greatest act of creation?

4.   Have you ever experienced evil? Describe.

IS MONEY THE ROOT OF ALL EVIL?

Many people besides my friend Janet have trouble with the idea of making money. They feel that money is the root of all evil. But if you read the Bible, you learn that jealousy and greed about money are the root of all evil. But understand that there are many kinds of "love" and many kinds of fascination with an object. You can "love" an object in the negative sense by being avaricious and possessive about it. Instead of you controlling that obsession, it controls you. That's not really love. To love is to love all of life and all of the manifestations of life, because all of life is a manifestation of your creator, which lives within you and within all things. If this is true, then there is no difference between a magnificent tree and a ten-dollar bill. Money has been manifested on the physical plane, just like that tree. It is manifested by the creator and should be honored in the same way. If the creator gives you the ability to make money and you throw that opportunity away, it is like tossing a religious icon at the wall so that it breaks into pieces. There really is no difference. There is as much of God in that icon as there is in a dollar bill. I know that some people will take issue with this. But if you understand that money is part of love, is part of a spiritual power that animates us all—if you can truly understand this— you must honor anything that is manifested by the creator. What is in front of you is presented by God for you to learn from. It is all a part of you. There is no separation. Our feelings of aloneness and separateness are really a part of the process of missing the mark. To claim our birthright—physical abundance and abundance of spirit—is to proclaim the ultimate goodness of all that is.

Ideas to Contemplate

1.   What is my current lesson in life?

2.   What is my biggest lesson in life?

3.   Who upsets me the most? That person is a good teacher for me.

9

Life and Life Force

If your every single breath became a prayer
You'd see atoms as angels and hear in each wind
The whir of Love's wings, and feel in each moment
The Beloved pulling you into His heart.

—Andrew Harvey, *Love's Glory: Re-Creating Rumi*

FLASH FLOOD

I walk often in the dry creek bed with my friend, the old
Indian wise woman named Twin Dreamers. One afternoon in
the winter, we had decided to meet at the river crossing by
Morning Star Road. On my drive there, bolts of lightning split
the darkening sky, and rain began to bounce off the dusty hood
of my truck. By the time I joined my friend, we stood on a high
boulder watching a flash flood coursing down from Elephant
Butte. The old woman pointed across the torrent of rushing
white water to the ledge where we usually sat and talked. It was
quickly becoming flooded with rainwater.

"The life blood of Mother Earth," Twin Dreamers said with a

broad smile, recalling our conversation of some months ago.

"If life's blood is love, then what do you think now about our creek?"

"Well, now all the rocks, the sand, and the trees are coming alive. There is movement. There will be new growth every-where."

"To me, it's like our very existence. We educate ourselves and even become masters. These stones are perfection in a way, but almost dormant, like the seeds deep underground in winter. Now the water comes, the nurturing, the moment-to-moment joy. The stones glisten in the light; the trees sprout. *To me, this surging river is the love. It's the greatest dream of power.* Power is like the riverbed; it must wait for the rain to restore its purpose. But we as humans can call in the rain, the love. We can move with the exquisite balance of love and power, if we choose."

"You cannot push the river" or force nature to do other than it will. But we, as conscious beings, can learn from the ebb and flow in nature as it relates to our own search for wisdom. I have experienced the life force within the powers of nature and the forces of consciousness within each of us to be complementary. I have found that the great unleashed energy in a flash of light-ning or a river flooding out of control can support and illumi-nate the energies within our own consciousness that we can learn to control. But understanding and a way of perceiving the process of our intellect are essential. How do we think? Each of us is unique and uses the energy of mind and thought in a dif-ferent way. I think we are also unaware of our great need for "deep time," a time symbolized by the way the sandy riverbed holds its power and seeds of life in a state of repose until the rains come. We, too, must invite the powers of the universe into our moments of "resonance" and contemplation, so the beauty that we are can sprout when a flood of energy comes, and the wisdom within us can be born.

VERTICAL CONSCIOUSNESS AND WISDOM

In the vertical movement and searching of our consciousness, we manifest inspiration into physical being. We conjure a book or a painting, and we create it. In stasis, however, we move into horizontal thought patterns, data, habits, technology, and group patterns, and we abandon inspiration, allowing fear and loneliness to paralyze us into a deathlike state of thoughtless repetitions of lifeless patterns. Mastery, which swirls through vertical consciousness and beckons us ever closer to God, is never found in stasis. Every cell in every living organism is filled with energy and movement. Since every cell of every living organism was created by and is intended to be filled with energy and creativity, when we are without vertical consciousness, the reaching up toward God, aesthetics, and inspiration, life is aborted.

The sacred dance of life, whether it be cellular or your own life force, is created by the female implosion of energy, or the pulling in of power that causes the stirring of life force, the receiving of inspiration and creativity, and the equal and opposite giving out or manifestation of the mirrors of consciousness in the male explosion of energy. If you position yourself in a place of technology, data, and horizontally derived information, instead of contemplation and moments of repose before a thing of beauty, whether nature or a work of art, life can never be fulfilling. You must also have the movement of the combined explosion and implosion of life force within both men and women and all forms of life to create vertical movement and a life of wisdom. Within this kind of understanding lies the possibility of mastery. Let me give you an example of how this process manifests in our lives.

I had spent several days camping in the Superstition Mountains of Arizona with my teacher, Agnes. The spring beauty of the wilderness had been breathtaking on every vista.

The scent of newborn grass, the reflections of sunlight off the crystal clear streams, the striations of purple, red, orange, and pink in the sky at sunset could not compare to the beauty of silence that surrounded us. We spent hours of "deep time" without speaking, resting in the grace and elegance of nature.

"Resonance—there is no wisdom without it. Resonance is a natural phenomenon, the shadow of import alongside the body of fact, and it cannot flourish except in deep time." I was reminded of a quote by Birkerts. How beautifully he describes the basic wisdom or search for completion in this life.

On my return to Phoenix, jolted back into hard reality, I met my friend Betty at a flourishing downtown restaurant. Betty seemed different. In comparison to the driving beat of music, and animated and well-dressed patrons, she seemed drab, her eyes almost hollow, her shoulders slumped, closing off the energy from her heart.

"Betty!" I reached out to touch her arm. "Are you feeling okay?"

"Yes . . . well, I guess I feel cut off from life—lonesome maybe," she said.

"What's happened?" I asked.

"I think maybe I'm addicted to my job. I'm on that computer twenty-four hours a day. I don't have a life anymore. Why do I feel so empty—I've never been more successful!"

"Are you still doing your spiritual work or hiking? Do you still ride your horse?" I asked.

"Heavens no! I don't have time for those things."

We spoke together for a long time that day. What Betty was describing to me was a technologically, data-based, information-filled life that was horizontal by nature. Her loneliness came from her lack of vertical consciousness. There is no wisdom or fulfillment in the contemplation of computers and data.

I work with so many people who are fascinated by the birth of our new technologies, but their lives are taken over by it. I fear for the loss of wisdom, the loss of aesthetics, the loss of our comprehension of beauty in all things. In beauty is truth. How can we know truth if we cannot see or comprehend beauty? Betty and I began to work together to reclaim her soul. It was hard for her, because something inside her akin to joie de vivre had gone to sleep. It was like uprooting an addiction, and a new sacred tree of life had to be planted and cultivated within her. A tree whose branches reached up toward the understanding of God and spirit. I have found that you almost need spiritual dynamite to move horizontal consciousness back to including vertical consciousness. A good balance between the two is fine, but very arduous to maintain. Perhaps this will be our challenge in the new millennium—cultivating wisdom and vertical consciousness in an ever-growing horizontally based techno-crazed world.

THE SACRED DANCE OF LIFE

The accumulation of information and spiritual life force are created within the human body by the implosion of energy. When you express your spirit through the translation of that information, movement is created in a spiraling form even within the cells of your body. Oftentimes, I call this the spiral dance of life. Let's talk about how this relates to personal power. When you have what looks like power in the world coming from a place of ego and false self, where competition and conquest are at the forefront, you may think that what you acquire will bring you happiness and peace. Instead, you are owned by the very possessions and ideals you thought would set you free. This is an implosion of energy without explosion. This is a kind of energetic holding pattern created by greed and possibly fear. A stasis is created and ultimately drains you of energy. You lose power. If you stay in that state of nonmovement long enough, the holding of energy can become the beginning of death. Move into the world with your acts of power from a place of expansion and explosion; expand your heart and your spirit because you want to leave the earth a better place than you found it. When your heart opens, your consciousness begins to move, and you will find that you like to work, you like to do things, and you like to accomplish because you enjoy the actual act of doing for itself and not necessarily for what it brings. Vertical thought is a way of bringing in spiritual abundance and will always bring you something in equal kind in terms of physical, worldly abundance. You achieve abundance because of the energy you are generating, but you don't do it from a place of materialism or greed. You do well and bring in abundance from a place of love. So again, love is at the base of creation.

For example, as she learned to think in a vertical way, reaching up toward spirit and inspiration, Betty realized on a very deep level that the great knowledge she gained on the computer was not anchored in actual physical experience. Betty realized that she had lost her point of view in life, and lost her love of life. So she remedied that by consciously experiencing vertical thought through the inspiration she received in nature. She began manifesting remarkable children's computer games, but games involving nature and beautiful ideas combined with poetry and art. Her point of view is now strong. She feels that life must be lived in balance. Computers are a magnificent tool, but they are just a tool. Betty is working on her personal relationships and is taking time for herself and for her spiritual growth.

MANIFESTING INSPIRATION

Goodness, integrity, and wisdom already exist within your spirit, but you must learn to access that consortium of wisdom.

Part of the challenge involves successfully managing the movement of your energy, again through vertical consciousness not
just horizontal.

Ideas to Contemplate

1.   How do you relate to the gifts you have been given by God?
     This is a very important aspect of who you are and how you
     see and define yourself.

2.   How do you find inspiration and manifest that inspiration into
     the world? Do you have a sense of reaching up to God and
     asking for inspiration?

3.   Do you sense the difference between vertical consciousness
     and your relationship to spirit and horizontal consciousness
     and the gathering of information?

4.   Is your heart open to your sense of power, to your sense of
     oneness with all of life?

5.   A person who manifests inspiration successfully moves from a
     position of spirit and strength. Do you do this? How?

   Choosing to move from a position of centeredness and power
in your life means choosing to move toward success, abundance, and fulfillment. This means that you have a relationship
with true power or power that comes down from spirit. It means
that you have made a place inside yourself for power to live
comfortably.
   Claiming your personal power means that you have dealt
with your fears of being seen and heard in the world. So many of
us hide most of our lives. I certainly did. Most people who have
been abused as children are afraid to be noticed. Unconsciously,
they think they'll be hit if they are seen. We hide in the secret

corners of our existence, because we are afraid to become visible, to become illuminated so that all can see who we are. We think that is a vulnerable and dangerous position; it was for me. Power was a choice, made with great intent and with great thought. Taking personal power oftentimes can be a gift, allowing you to put your charisma on display. But to be truly powerful is not only to be charismatic, but to be a master of whatever you do. When we hide from power, we hide from abundance. We hide from love.

WELCOMING ABUNDANCE

If you have chosen to live from a position of true personal power, you will naturally accept abundance into your life to nourish your love-power connection. God, or the Great Spirit, is the life force of creation. I see this life force as a grand energy that lives within us all, but it must be recognized and honored. Life force is the creation of substance, and you can learn to help choreograph the manifestation of this substance through your vertical thoughts and through love. I don't want all this to sound complicated. In reality, these concepts are very natural and simple.

Let's talk about love for a moment. In love, you open your heart to the radiance of this life force, and within you is created a magnificent magical child or source of power that begins to have a life of its own. I call this power a magical child, because this force needs to be properly guided and educated with the focus of your will. With the strength of your intent and point of view, you can create power in your life and manifest your dreams. Many people I work with have asked me this question in one form or another: "How do you maintain the extraordinary radiance of love in your life and balance love with power and success? At the beginning stirrings of power, how do you keep spiritual food coming back into your life through your daily efforts? How do you maintain the glow of love and power and spirit all together?" Well, first of all, you start with the connection between God and the love in your heart. You have understood this with the concept of vertical consciousness. When you open to that creative force, you also open to abundance. Spiritual abundance is related to a blissful state of physical radiance and personal power that glows throughout your entire body. This power is recognized by other people as an irresistible pull, which they may call charisma. You know what the pull is, but they aren't sure why they're attracted to you.

Have you ever fallen in love? You walk down the street, and suddenly all of those people who haven't noticed you for years are staring at you and noticing you and asking you out—because you are so radiant. You glow in the dark, and people want to be next to your light. Abundance works the same way. Suddenly things are coming to you. You feel like you are on a roll. You have the Midas touch. You can't do anything wrong. Is this a coincidence, an accident? I don't think so. It's a state of being. You can move into that state of being through your will. But there is one thing that the will cannot do. It cannot create the gratefulness that is needed to make abundance a part of your life. Love begins to grow and deepen within you when you take time to recognize the beauty and magic of life. Take time to read. Take time to dream.

There was a great wise old grandmother whom I was fortunate enough to spend time with the year before she passed on. She lived in northern New Mexico and loved to have me take her for drives on the dirt back roads in my dilapidated old red pickup truck. I laid towels over the broken springs of the seats to make her more comfortable. One summer evening we drove southwest of Taos into the orange and red setting sun, dust billowing out behind us. She knew she was dying and she wanted me to understand things before she left. So she would talk to me as we bumped down the road, knowing I wouldn't argue much because I was too busy keeping the balding tires out of the deep ruts. I used to wonder how I could hear her soft gentle voice so perfectly over the clamor of rattling, rusted fenders and doors.

"For there to be an abundant state of being in your life, Lynn, you must move from an understanding of the inexplicable connection between your heart and the splendor of the Great Spirit. To link your open heart," she placed her fist over her heart, "and the substance of life force energy," she pointed toward the setting sun, "you must create a bridge, a kind of energy line. You can see this bridge coming from your heart as a beautiful, radiant energy line that is luminous and shining like that sun. It extends from your heart to the creative force of life. You see that force like golden light moving through that line and filling your heart and your body with a sense of richly glowing fullness. But it is your gratefulness that creates this possibility. Remember, Lynn, it is the gratefulness that brings you closer to God. And it is the gratefulness that recognizes and thanks God and all of the forces of creative life for being there within you. I have always felt this, and I know you have, too. Then your light begins to grow. Your light is irresistible. How can you take your eyes off that sunset?"

"I know," I said as the truck lurched into a pothole.

"Light is irresistible to money, irresistible to love, and irresistible to power. You have heard that old saying that may even be older than me," she giggled. "God is made of light. I believe that this is true on both a symbolic level and on a real level. I think the manifestation of light in this world is what keeps the forces of darkness at bay. The forces of darkness are all around us and have a real life and form. But they aren't created out there by somebody else; they are created by you and me. Our true war is not outside us; it is within us and around our own weaknesses. There is nothing in this life that is separate from you.

Everything is a part of you. So when your friends become abundant and open their hearts to the light of existence and creativity, it becomes easier for you to open your heart and your sense of expansion, so that abundance can live within you as well. It's so silly for people to be envious and jealous. If you do well, then I can do well, because we are part of each other, as it should be."

As often would happen after she had been talking a while, Grandmother would look to the horizon and the setting sun as if she felt it were beckoning her to follow.

THE FOUR PRINCIPLES OF ABUNDANCE

To put all of this in a context that is even clearer, you might want to think in terms of four basic principles of abundance. Let me explain.

The first principle relating to the energy of abundance is to trust in the universe to provide you with exactly what you need, not only to live, but also to enlighten you on your path toward self-realization and mastery. *Each experience in your life is a teacher, holding a mirror up to you so you can learn.* If you do not use your work or business or relationship as a mirror for your process of growth, then you are missing so much of what your daily life has to offer.

The second principle of abundance is to understand the unlimited opportunities there are to learn in this life. In the great mystery of life, an infinite abundance of spirit and health and remuneration are available to you if you are open to receiving this plenitude.

The third principle of abundance is to cultivate gratefulness. If you express your gratefulness in ways large and small, then the abundance of the universe will begin to flow through you because you have developed a direct relationship with God or the Great Spirit.

The fourth principle of abundance is love. You have to love the process both of earning money and of giving it away. If you love the process, both of earning the money to buy what is necessary as well as to serve the people who come to you for your services, then you are engaged in a process of love. Life is a process of expansion within your mind and within your heart, and abundance will be yours.

When you consider these four principles of abundance, you see that even seeking material abundance is a spiritual pursuit. It may look like a physical pursuit in that you are defining a product or service and then presenting that product or service for sale, but at its essence, it's a process of love. Every aspect of this process of love is an expression of gratefulness, of trusting that what you need will be there for you, of trusting that the Great Spirit is watching over you with universal abundance and giving you what you need for a radiant and prosperous future.

Ideas to Contemplate

1. Do you agree that seeking abundance is a spiritual pursuit? Why or why not?

2. Do you trust in spirit to provide for you?

3. Name four acts of gratefulness you can perform every day.

Mastery

Can you nurture your souls by holding them
in unity with the One?
Can you focus your ch'i—your energy
and become as supple, as yielding as a baby?
Can you clear your mind of all its dross
without throwing out the Tao with it?
Can you do it without self-interest
so you shine like a diamond?
Can you love the people of your nation
without being pulled into action?
Can you turn yourself around
and let Her rise up over you?
The world spans out in four directions—
and can you be as embracing?
Birthing, nurturing and sustaining:
the Tao does this unceasingly . . .
It gives without holding on to what it has made.
It gives everything essence, without reward
It knows, without flaunting it
It is serene, beyond desiring
—and this is its Virtue and its Source.

—TAO TE CHING

10

The Essence of Mastery

Only in our doing can we grasp
  you.
Only with our hands can we
  illumine you.
The mind is but a visitor:
it thinks us out of our world.
Each mind fabricates itself.
We sense its limits, for we have
  made them.

And just when we would flee them,
  you come
and make of yourself an offering.
I don't want to think a place for you.
Speak to me from everywhere.
Your Gospel can be comprehended
without looking for its source.
When I go toward you
it is with my whole life.

—RAINER MARIA RILKE

Controlling others is not power. Control is laying your reality over someone else's. Power is holding strength with open hands.

A CONVERSATION WITH JULIA

Julia and I were having one of our usual discussions about life over lunch one day in New York.

"I think that balance in your life has a lot to do with your personal ethics," she said. Julia had become a doctor in her thirties and had specialized in cancer. She had long black hair to her shoulders, and looked elegant in her Armani suit.

"What is your definition of ethics?" I asked, nodding to the waitress as she brought my chicken salad.

"I can't offer you a precise definition. But I believe ethics is related to the development of the soul."

"Do you mean the soulful ethics within your life? Or do you mean right and wrong medical ethics and so forth?"

"I mean what's hard and what's not hard. If I work diligently, I can make money easily, but it's hard to stay in touch with my soul and that sense of inner truth when I see so much pain and suffering. Somehow it comes down to my instinct of what's healthy or not healthy for me. I can't be there for people if I don't take care of myself, and that is hard for me to remember. What's healthy is not always easy. A simple example would be exercise. A more difficult example would be giving up an addictive relationship." I smiled with great love and respect for Julia, who was currently living through a hellish breakup of a long-term relationship.

For a split second, a song playing in the background held a drumbeat that reminded me of a Native American ceremony. For a moment, I saw Julia as she might have been in another lifetime. Her long black hair brushed her waist as she swayed and danced in a buckskin dress with bright red beads that glinted in the firelight. How simple life was back then, how uncomplicated in terms of your role in the tribe. How difficult if nature went against you and food was scarce. Everyone knew what was easy and hard—your tasks, making shelter, caring for the children and your spirit. Survival was a huge part of life. You had to hunt and pick for almost every meal. Now we have supermarkets and complications and sophistication. We have so much ease and so much confusion. I could almost smell the fire and hear the dreams of a young native woman whispered on the north wind. I was suddenly brought back to the present as a waiter dropped a load of dishes onto the floor, smashing them into a thousand pieces. I looked at Julia, blinking away my thoughts as I listened to her.

"In your book *Dark Sister,* Lynn, you spoke of an ancient legend memorized by your native teachers. It is said by some Tibetan masters, aborigines, and Native Americans that most of the great knowledge that is on this planet came originally from an intelligent source on the Pleiades. They say we work on different levels and different dimensions of existence—the astral, etheric, and in our dreams—to find wisdom, to develop our God-being within us. Depending on what it is we need to understand, we move out to different energy fields to learn. Dreaming is one energy level and meditation is another, both different from our everyday life. You know, Lynn," Julia said, taking a bite of broiled salmon, "when I look into a microscope and see the worlds of life, tiny microscopic galaxies of swirling existence, I cannot deny the massive intelligence that abides beyond our normal vision. Maybe the universe of which the ancient legends speak is within the interior of our own energy field."

"If the Pleiades is the mother of wisdom and 'we are made from stars, and to the stars we must one day return,' perhaps these legends among ancient peoples apply to each and every person on the planet, and perhaps they provide a map to mastery. What do you think about such ideas?" I asked, sipping a cafe au lait.

"I have a very simple vision of how to get to mastery. I see myself as aware of where I am now, where I have to go, and how to get there. Becoming a doctor, I found a way to reach my goal, which was mastering techniques. Now I'm going from the place where I was to the place where the new part of my path is. Now, as in the ancient teachings you work with, I want to make my work an art balanced by love—personal love. But I have to find the right questions, such as 'Does this area of my work still serve me and others? Am I going in a correct direction in order to keep evolving?' As long as I am able to do that with every obstacle and everything that I have to learn, as long as I can see my life as a divine, mysterious challenge, in the end I know I will find mastery."

"What is the key? Is there a key, like love and power? How does that key affect your concept of mastery?" I asked. "I think perhaps the balance of love and power *is* the key. If you have power in life, but you don't have love, you're miserable, as you know. But yet, how can you have love if you're powerless? If you're powerless, I don't know if you can love yourself," I added, leaning back in my chair.

"I think of myself as a very powerful person. I know that I have a lot of strength. I just have the feeling that even though I have this power, I am still in the dark because I have yet to balance my power equally with love. I have these feelings about where I have to go, but so often I am just too blind to see the directions. Somehow illuminations come to me in the process of making choices and I see that there is a part of me who is afraid to become what I'm trying to become. Being aware of my choices helps me, especially when I'm deeply involved in my work. It's funny, isn't it, Lynn? *But the greatest moments of illumination come when you least expect it, maybe when you're on the freeway, and almost never when you are looking for them.*"

"Yes, yes, Julia." We hugged each other. "It's the process, the doing, the magnificent, innocent, spontaneous process. To me it's like taking a walk in the desert at dawn. First light peeks across the McDowell Mountains, and there is nothing you can do to stop the sun, the illumination of dew on a cactus flower, and you're filled with gratefulness in your heart for the grace of life. It's so simple, Julia, so overwhelming. Why can't we just let enlightenment happen, like the sun coming up over the horizon? So we continue to balance our lives and search our souls for truth."

THE NATURE OF MASTERY

Mastery is the process of weaving the pragmatic threads of technique—the physical, technical work that helps us gather power—with the shining fibers of love, the dimensions of spirit. Love and power are not opposites; they are different aspects of the same whole. Recognizing this, living this, is true mastery. When we are able to see the possibility of balancing love with power in a moving, shifting manifestation of reality, then we create the access to a life of joy.

As I wrote earlier, always remember that the situation or person who has the ability to upset you the most, to pull you off center the most, can be your greatest teacher, particularly in the attainment of mastery. Once you have reached true mastery, a state of continuing peace and freedom, you can sit at the center of your own being, feeling the world and nature and the harmonies of all existence moving around you. They affect you if you choose, and they do not affect you if you choose. But you must never do less than your job or position in life requires. When your employees do less and not more, your company will fail. When you are lazy and do less than required, your life will fail.

As you search for more ways to do well and become greater than intended, you help us evolve as a species. You sit in a position of ultimate efficiency, being larger and more full of life force than was originally intended for your position, witnessing all that surrounds you with great clarity. You are simply at the still point, an inner place of pure existence, with chaos all around you but not touching you. When you are in your power, you have released your need for constant distraction from your center. You function every day with an intensity where you do all you can do in your position and more. You never leave anything untended. You have released your need for addictions. You have become master of your own life. You have become the prime mover around which all else achieves a higher state of functioning.

In mastery, you are aware of all of your abilities and because you function within every task, holding complete attention and power, no task is too small or meaningless. I remember an incident with my teacher, Agnes Whistling Elk, that taught me that no task is too small to practice your ability to do something in a sacred and perfect way. Agnes and I were washing dishes in her cabin. Agnes held a dirty dish up to a shaft of sunlight and then handed it to me. I took it and sloshed water and soap on it as I peered out the window. Agnes gave me a shove, and the dish slipped out of my fingers and splintered on the floor.

"No!" she said. "Let's try again." She handed me another dish and said, "Do as I do." Agnes picked up a dish as if it were a sacred object. "Hold your dish as if it were part of the Great Spirit, which it is. Touch it as if it is the skin of a newborn baby, carefully and with your full attention." She began to move the soapy sponge on the surface of the dish. "Now glide your hand and wash, staying aware of the sacred circle of life. Remember all things are sacred and part of God. Would you wash the face of God while staring out the window? *The greatest things in your life happen in a moment. If you are not in the moment, you miss everything.*"

When you approach life from this stance, you know that you have done your homework. You realize that on every level of existence your techniques are in order, that you have the tools necessary to survive magnificently in your world because you polish and perfect them every day. You love yourself for your abilities as well as for your flaws. *In mastery, you become aware of a different kind of light. That light is a reflection of the flaws of your being, as if a rainbow prism of light were reflecting off a crack in a crystal. It is within the flaws of your being that mastery is found.* Those flaws are gateways. You face them, walk through them, and learn the lessons you came here to learn. Being able to own and love all aspects of yourself, even those places within yourself that seem darkest and most ineffectual, is the art of true mastery. Healing those aspects and filling your darkness with an excess of light is how you evolve to a higher state of being. Staying centered within your own house of mirrors demonstrates the true manifestation of mastery.

BALANCING EMOTIONS AND THE MIND

Finding mastery also means that you have learned to balance your emotions. We are often afraid of empowering ourselves, and we sabotage our efforts at the last moment before we graduate or attain our goal. Balancing your emotions with your mental acumen brings transformation and allows you to manifest your ideas of your true worth in life. You must become a greater person. A greater light must radiate from you than was originally intended. In this way, you grow and become more successful.

What does transformation mean in your emotional makeup? When you're in your power, you're in control of your emotions. Your emotions are not controlling you. When you are truly experiencing love and allowing love to live in your heart, you have a great understanding of your own emotions. Your light, your fullness ever extends its boundaries, and you share it without fear. You are acting in your life instead of reacting to old conditioning and old ideas that no longer serve you.

Men and women often cope differently with mind and emotions. Women, by and large, have difficulty taking form in life, or defining their identity to themselves or others. Ask a woman how she would like to be portrayed on the front of *Time* magazine and what the caption under her photograph would read. This would mean that she has accomplished something really

wonderful and powerful in life. Many women, lacking a compre-
hensive vision, will answer this question by saying something a
bit vague, such as, "I would like to bring beauty into life." And I
would reply, "Once you understand *how* you're going to bring
that beauty into life, once you give form to that beauty, then
please tell me, and describe yourself, because then I will know
how to assist you."

Most men, on the other hand, take form and describe themselves very easily. They take an identity in the world—"I'm a
lawyer" or "I'm a professor"—because that is, by and large, what
is expected of them in this society. Taking form and being clear
about your identity means that you balance your mind and emotions, including emotions about how you accept yourself, how
you relate to other people, how you feel about the most important things in your society. Your form also has to do with how
you think about money, abundance, relationships, your own
body, and the pragmatic things of life as well as the sacred
things. The way you express your emotions and intellect has a
great deal to do with how you manifest love, power, and your
purpose in the world.

Mastery requires the balance of both your feelings and your
intellect. A good way to talk about balancing your mind and
emotions is to imagine a man and a woman in a relationship.
Think of my young friends Mary and Jack. Mary is a woman
who lives for the most part in her emotions. She met and fell in
love with Jack, a man who lives for the most part in his mind.
This is predominantly how most men and women are. Jack and
Mary got together and there was incredible attraction between
them, which in actuality came from the merging of spirit within
them, from the heart and spirit that was manifested in their
attraction. But it was neither emotional nor mental. It was spiritual in nature because when you are in love, you are totally in
the moment, expressing the deepest part of your soul. When

Jack and Mary came together, they made love, and they physically joined together in the bonding process of marriage. After they married, things changed, as they often do, and the pragmatic aspects of life crept in. I found Mary talking about what she felt about what Jack thought. Jack talked about what he thought about what Mary felt. They did not bring inspiration into their discussions. There was no more spiritual insight in their discussions. They only argued about the physical aspects of life. They talked about taking out the garbage and dealing with bills, and occasionally they made love. I'm making a generality, but what was left out of their circle of creativity was spirit. When spirit is left out of any relationship, including our relationship with ourselves, the relationship will eventually die. And it loses love, absolutely. It loses its power, absolutely.

I helped Jack and Mary reclaim spirit in their lives, by teaching them how to do a simple sacred ceremony once a week where they spoke with a talking stick between them that they had chosen and decorated with special items. "You can only speak the truth across this stick," I said. This led them into prayer and meditation. They began backpacking and exploring the beauty of nature. The Great Spirit gives you your soul, but you have to make the first step to experience it.

Jack came to me one day, and he said, "Across the landscape of my imagination is my mental attitude and the way that I use my mind. I need to learn more about how I think about things. Am I logical? Am I disciplined? How do I think about love? What do I think about power? Am I coherent in the way that I find answers to my problems, especially with Mary?" he asked.

"When you discover your thought processes, then you'll discover your wisdom. What triggers your imagination, Jack, and how do you define your emotions? The mind is very tricky and seductive. The mind is the finest tool that we have as human beings. But the mind is programmable. It is something that can be conditioned and refined. The mind, however, can make you believe that you are that—that you are your mind. That's your problem, and that is a misconception. It is important for you to learn to balance your thinking with your emotions so that the relationship between these two spheres of energy called Mary and Jack is balanced and harmonious. Start asking your heart what it feels instead of asking your intellect. This is your path to harmony," I said.

CREATING A LIFELINE

For all of us, mastery at first represents an unknown world. When moving into the unknown, I am often reminded of a deep-sea diver going beneath the surface of the sea for the first time. When you move into uncharted territories, like the bottom of the sea, you need to take a lifeline to survive. The lifeline is something that is familiar. It is something that you can take with you, something that makes you feel secure in an unknown world. When you move into the fine art of mastery, you need to take your techniques with you. The techniques that you have learned are your lifeline; they are what is familiar in an otherwise alien world. These techniques are what you've learned about functioning in different capacities in your life. These techniques are precious to you because they make you capable and efficient. As you become highly efficient, your techniques can transform into a kind of love and appreciation for what you accomplish. It is then that you begin to move to a higher and more powerful experience.

Mastery becomes the bridge between love and power. *Mastery is the result of love and power, and it is also the bridge between them.* Mastery is dynamic and ever moving and ever changing. It is not a state of inertia. It is not stasis. It is constant movement. It is a way of being. Finding mastery involves journeying between technique and art, between beauty and truth, between power and love.

MOMENTS OF POWER, MOMENTS OF MASTERY

So often I have found that as people begin performing their acts of power, they forget that the beauty of life is in the not doing as well as the doing. One aspect of true mastery lies in that still point in the eye of a storm. When you stand at the center of a storm, untouched by the tumultuous wind swirling around you, a collecting begins. You begin to collect the available energy and store it inside you to use later. It is similar to a healer gathering the forces of nature and choreographing them into the process of healing. In focusing only on your technique, however, you miss the greatest moment of power that is hidden behind all activity. Power is held in the silences and the stillness. When you pull back a bow or compress a coiled spring, there is a moment of stillness before the release. Power is found in that moment. *Whether pulling back the bow and aiming your arrow or using techniques in your everyday work, there is power in the waiting.* The simple stance of considering and cultivating a tremendously heightened state of awareness allows you to gather great power. This can happen in a simple meeting with others where you listen intently and then speak at just the right moment so that your impact is tremendous.

You need to know how to recognize a moment of power when it comes to you, to begin to know the difference between the tremendous power and charisma of certain acts and the openings that are created by waiting and becoming receptive to the energies that come to you. You can learn to move through these openings and captivate a situation.

At the moment of stillness, always remember there come flashes or quiet moments of realization that curl around you like the fog at dawn, and they must be received by you as a womb receives the seed of life. You cannot "push the river." You cannot force yourself to be happy. *You cannot make magical events occur. They come to you as a gift, and they are shared with you by the Great Spirit and the powers of all the sacred beings that surround you.* It is a sacred dance that goes on and on forever, but you may be unaware of it because you don't yet know how to listen and to see.

And how do you learn how to see and to listen? By getting back to the tiny moments that go unnoticed in most everyone's life. By observing how others move, seeing how they close their heart by slumping their shoulders, and you come to know that they are closed to you. By sensitizing your antenna, mainly by listening to what people really say and how they say it. Use your magnificent body, which is one of your finest instruments through exercise or yoga, and ask your body how it feels about events in your life. Cool your mind with a preponderance of small and sacred moments. Listen to nature and the sounds of the wind. Place your hand on a large stone and ask it to tell you about time and its dominion over your life. By heightening your abilities to hear and taste and smell and sense with all that you are, you become part of your environment, and nature becomes a living part of you.

So push the envelope of your existence gently, carefully. Hold your power for the right moment, and listen to the whisperings of the beauty that surrounds you, and you will hold the keys of the gateway to your path of heart.

As a society, we tend to identify with the technique, with *what* we do. My teacher Agnes Whistling Elk once asked me, "And what have you learned, my daughter, from all the work that we have done together?"

I was very excited and said, "Well, I have learned to be a healer. I have learned to do acts of power in the world, and I am an author."

"No, my daughter," she admonished, "you are a woman living her truth who happens to write, who happens to heal and work with people."

I had to laugh, because she had definitely caught me off guard. I know this fact to be true, and yet I fell into thinking that I am what I do. *It is so easy to lose yourself in the process of technique, so easy to forget who you are.*

Life is a process of remembering your original nature, remembering why you were born, and remembering who you truly are— that you are here to become one with your god in this lifetime, if you choose. The essence of the work you do is what you want to experience. *When you focus your intent by working well, you find a beautiful sense of wholeness.* It is the essence and the heart of your focus that produces efficiency, and all efficient acts are successful. In the circling and the stalking of spiritual knowledge and wisdom, you will produce efficient acts that are successful because they will be balanced by a sense of spirit and a supreme power. But even in your success, prepare yourself to listen. *Listen as you circle and stalk; wait for a moment when stillness comes and you stand in honor of the heart of the moment.* Then power will rise and present itself to you in a process of new beginnings. Power comes in movement. Once you complete an efficient act, you go on to the next. It is within this wisdom that we all need to move and become aware with our heightened sensitivities.

We look for the grand moments, the great cataclysms, the great shocking show of sparks and fire and flame and explosions of energy to feel successful and powerful, and we tend to forget the preponderance of the small, mysterious moments. We miss the magic that is being presented to us because we are going too fast, because we are looking for something larger. It is essential to remember that everyone and everything is your teacher, if you will only look at the person and the situation that you're involved in with openness and understanding.

I learned so much the other day from a gas station attendant. Two gang members wandered in and tried to pick a fight with him while he was cleaning some spilled gas off the side of my truck. They yelled insults at him for being sloppy and stupid. The attendant laughed and made a joke. When it became obvious that there would be no fight, the kids left.

"Do you think you should call the police? Those kids looked like they were very threatening and could be trouble," I said.

"You're right, but couldn't you feel their pain? If I can help it, why would I want to add to their pain?"

"I see what you mean," I said, surprised at his compassion and understanding. As I drove off I thought about how many confrontations could be avoided if we used our creativity in a potentially difficult situation, the way the gas station attendant had just done. He had held a lot of power and presence as he faced those gang kids.

Know that all of life is your mirror and that every situation contains a lesson for you—a challenge in some way where your consciousness can become wrapped around that moment and a new vision can be brought to life. Once you live this, you will enter the fulfillment of mastery.

PARADISE ON EARTH

I don't think there's anyone who doesn't yearn to find the way home. But home, as I have learned from my teachers, is the sacred garden of our own spirit—that place of serenity within each of us. You don't find paradise "out there." Paradise is a world where we live in the center of our own reality, knowing who we are. Doubt is nonexistent here because you've worked hard and felt the results. Confusion is long gone because you've dared to open your heart and experience love. This is where we all want to live, but you won't get there without efficient effort and the understanding of your own spirit. This is where balance and harmony are wed, where we feel happy and at peace. We've created mirrors in life—relationships, work, and ideas—and we learned from them. In this world of mastery, we are not afraid to take risks, to love one another, and to follow our dreams.

With power, you find a way to manifest those dreams into life. Mastery and the balance that you hold within your being of power and love create the access to a life of peace and freedom. With love in your heart, you have learned how to sustain your daily accomplishments. Love is how you maintain this ecstatic experience. When your dreams come true, you're living in paradise. When you have achieved mastery, you are dreaming—and living—for the good of all.

Ideas to Contemplate

1. List four small events that brought magic into your life.

2. How do you balance love and power in life?

3. Think of two events where you could have shifted a confrontation. How could you have achieved this?

11

Pulling Back the Bow

You too will find your strength.
We who must live in this time
cannot imagine how strong you
   will become—
how strange, how surprising,
yet familiar as yesterday.
We will sense you
like a fragrance from a nearby
   garden
and watch you move through our
   days

like a shaft of sunlight in a
   sickroom.
We will not be herded into
   churches,
for you are not made by the
   crowd,
you who meet us in our solitude.
We are cradled close in your
   hands—
and lavishly flung forth.

—RAINER MARIA RILKE

THE METAPHOR OF ARCHERY

One beautiful, sunny morning as I was practicing with my bow and arrow, I became captivated by the sun shining on the polished wood of the bow. The grain of the wood became illuminated and obviously strong and perfectly formed. I have often used the metaphor of archery as an example of the nature of claiming your power and assuming mastery. That morning I became more aware than ever of the power symbolism has for all of us. As an archer I face my target, and I work to perfect my art. I hold in my hand the bow and arrow, or symbolically the tools of my trade. I aim at my target, or the symbol for the mastery of my art form, and I pull back the bow.

For you, imagine your target for a moment as your personal temple of power. How do you see your temple? What are the walls made of? Perhaps they are made of all the acts you are trying to accomplish. What are the elements contained in the temple? How would you define your tools of power? What are your objects of worship, and who are your teachers? For example, if you wanted to be an opera singer, perhaps your target would be perfecting a magnificent aria from *Madame Butterfly*. By keeping your eye on the target, the aria itself, you will steadily move toward your goal. If the walls of your temple are constructed from the high notes of music that are demanded of you, how do you enter the temple? By pulling back the bow and aiming. In this case, pulling back the bow would be finding the proper coach and then practicing your scales every day, working to perfect your craft by singing the most difficult notes over and over. After a while you have gotten closer to mastering the technique, and you are almost ready to let the arrow fly. However, there still is one thing missing that will determine the difference between missing or hitting your mark.

If you do not love what you are creating, power or technique alone will not do the job. If you have gathered power, contained it within you, and your heart is still closed, you will have stopped the flow of spirit, and there will never be enough energy to hit the mark. You might be able to sing the notes, but no one in the audience will care because you will not touch them. On the other hand, if you open your heart and then pull back the bow with centeredness and balance, you will be on your way. You will stay focused, take a deep breath, and let it fly. Surely then, your arrow will be ready to soar through the air and nail the target dead center. Your audience will be nourished by your expression, and you will have nourished yourself as well. Everyone wins. You will have added more beauty to the world. You will have reached a state of mastery by realizing the balance between love and power.

So how have you pulled back the bow in your life? Maybe for years and years, you pulled back the bow by educating yourself, dealing with the conditioning of your early family life, and healing your wounds—those places of fear and mistrust and ill health within your consciousness. You've arrived with very special abilities to live in an ecstatic and powerful way. Pulling back the bow has to do with choosing a target, but not aiming until you know you can hit your mark.

Pulling back the bow is a metaphor for doing the work, engaging in the movement and the flow that leads us to our goal. That happens when you have done your homework, your preparation. Although homework, preparation, and training your relationship with power is different for each of us, it always entails education and practice of some sort. For you, this may mean attending classes, or it may mean working as an apprentice, studying the lessons or techniques that will build the foundation for mastery. In order to transform your work into a nourishing art form, you need to include the creative element, the part that contains the spark of love. That spark of love is ignited by the passion you have for what you do—your chosen target. It is your passion that drives your intent and keeps you going through the hard times.

BECOMING CONNECTED TO ALL OF LIFE

The concept of power has to do with arriving at a goal and still remaining whole as a person, not giving away aspects of yourself for gain, but holding yourself together. At this point you have developed a trust in your ability to perform well, and your trust includes the knowledge that there is a spiritual core to your being, however you choose to define it. As you claim your power in a personal and beautiful way, your heart is full. You are becoming aware of the nature of trust. You realize that there is divine guidance in your life, and you trust the light and the inspiration that is flowing into you in so many ways. The spirit is coming to you through the efficiency in your efforts, your creative expression, your focus, your intent, your truth. The gratefulness that is filling you with happiness is the bridge you are creating between yourself and the higher power in the universe. You are becoming connected to all of life. You know who you are, and you will reach goals that have been out of reach, perhaps for your whole life. When you reach your goal, you are still a balanced person.

If you feel suddenly that you are losing your balance, moving out of your center, or giving away aspects of yourself, you are losing your personal power. You are probably aiming at the wrong target. You may wonder, How did this happen? Identifying this mistake may be one of the most important events in your life and may literally save your life. See this problem as a gift and ask yourself these questions.

Ideas to Contemplate

1. Has the activity I'm involved in outlived its usefulness?

2. Am I doing what I want to do or what someone else wants me to do—for example, my parents, my friends, or my mate?

3. Am I seeing my life through my own eyes or someone else's?

It is difficult to change your course, but if it is the wrong course, changing can be a great relief. It is an opportunity to stop for a while and move back into a process of self-searching until you find the passion within you that yearns for expression. When you find that you want that opportunity passionately, whether it be a relationship or some professional goal, you must learn to make yourself open to success.

In some ways, this is like stalking a rare bird, like a photographer seeking a storm eagle. When you move toward a certain opportunity in your life, and you want this opportunity passionately, you must learn to make yourself receptive. In other words, if you are going to stalk a rare bird, you first learn where the bird feeds, on what side of the mountain, and at what time of day. You find out when it goes into mating season, when it rests. You become the bird before you ever photograph the bird.

It is the same in our society. Before you ever get that position on Wall Street, you must set the arrow in your bow and aim. You must become ready for the position. You must become receptive to your prey. You make a place inside you for the power of that endeavor to live within you. You make a place within you that is attractive to whatever those energies might be that are outside you. Each profession, each relationship, has an energy of its own. Like is attracted to like, so for that energy to become part of you, you have to develop within yourself the ability to attract and absorb it.

If you want to become a lawyer, for example, you will surround yourself with all aspects of the law. You will study law, and you will become a part of the legal world long before you ever enter the courtroom as an attorney.

Everyone in life is unique. What is power for one person may not be power for another, so take some time and ask yourself these questions.

Ideas to Contemplate

1. What is power made of for you? Is it your beauty, your abilities, your age?

2. How do you define power?

3. How do you get power into your life? Name four ways (study, etc.).

4.   How do you project power into your relationships (through
     your talents, control issues, etc.)?

   Answering these questions for yourself is part of the process
of pulling back the bow. Projecting power into your life is shoot-
ing the arrow after you have pulled back the bow and secured
your intent and your vision. When you know where you are
going, when you know your target, you envision it with the
proper amount of intent, power, and energy behind your arrow.
Then you shoot your arrow with a centeredness, a balance, and
a state of perfection within your own mind and heart. Then,
surely, you will hit your target. Then, your arrow will fly
through the air with due speed, and you will be at the point of
realizing power and fulfillment in your life.
   So choose your target, but don't shoot until you know you
can hit it. This happens only after you have understood the
foundation of your power, which will be evident in the radiance
of your spirit. *Sitting still within the glow of your own well-being
and simplicity illuminates the environment around you.* That
bright swirl of action needs no response from anyone to manifest fully as a moment of splendor. Now shoot the arrow and
watch it fly, perfectly and gracefully, home.

Ideas to Contemplate

1.   Describe the most radiant person you have ever met.

2.   What is there in you that is like that person? How could you
     become more radiant?

12

Collaborating with Death

I love the dark hours of my being.
My mind deepens into them.
There I can find, as in old letters,
the days of my life, already lived,
and held like a legend, and
  understood.
Then the knowing comes: I can open
to another life that's wide and
  timeless.

So I am sometimes like a tree
rustling over a grave site
and making real the dream
of the one its living roots
embrace:
a dream once lost
among sorrows and songs.

—RAINER MARIA RILKE

FACING THE REALITY OF DEATH

The gift of life is *intimately interwoven with the reality of* death. True mastery depends not only on an appreciation of the principles of living, but on an awareness of our ultimate destiny. From the moment we are born into this world, we must face the fact that we will one day die. To accept this truth, to work with it daily, and to finally collaborate with it represents the ultimate form of mastery. Truly, there is no better way to demonstrate the mastery of life than in the quality of a person's death.

The fear of death is really the only one true fear in life. Death is a concept that most of us would rather not discuss, and yet, if we can make death our ally, we become invincible because then we have nothing to lose. We are no longer afraid, even of losing our own lives. If we can instill this kind of confidence in our- selves, then death will never take us at an unfortuitous time. We are already prepared.

Not long ago, I was sitting around a campfire with one of my teachers, Twin Dreamers, who is an elder woman from Panama, south of Mexico. I had been thinking about death and wanted to ask her about my confusion.

"Twin Dreamers, what is the relationship between intent and death?" I asked.

Twin Dreamers often teaches through humor. She chuckled as she scanned my serious face with her piercing eyes, which were reflecting the glow of the flames. She sat like a panther in repose. She picked up a twig and began switching it back and forth, almost like a cat's tail.

"Good question," she said. "The subject of death is inhabited by fear for most people. Intent wipes away fear."

I stared at her, thinking and watching the tiny mirrors sewn on her red and pink dress, shining like so many stars that had fallen to earth.

"Will," I finally asked, "is different from intent, isn't it?"

"How?" she asked, still flicking the stick.

"Will is potential, your conception of where you want to go. Intent, to me, is the application of that potential."

"Correct," the old woman said as she nodded, her brown skin lined from years of being in the sun. "*So many people with talent who don't apply themselves—what is that but the failure of intent?* Now, to answer your question," Twin Dreamers lay the twig down on the ground in a vertical position, "this represents the vertical concept or the picture that you have of what you want to accomplish." Then she picked up another stick, touched it to her forehead, and then placed it in a horizontal position. "This represents the doing of your picture. The sticks are crossed in perfect balance. There's your mastery."

"But what about death and intent?" I asked again.

"You see, little one, intent is full. When you are living in your center, your intent, there is no room for fear or cowardice. *Cowardice is the enemy of mastery.*"

I stared into her eyes again for a long time. "You say mastery—you mean, then, that to have a conscious death your intent must be mastered perfectly so that there is no fear in you."

"Exactly. It is all a perfect circle. Vertical thought is the picture, your dream. Horizontal consciousness is the doing of your dream, neither of which can happen without intent and the love of spirit. It's really so simple."

A few months later, I was riding a horse that had frightened me in the past. He was big and wild. After my learning with Twin Dreamers, I rode him differently. I focused my intent instead of worrying about what the he might do, such as buck. From my intent, the horse gained confidence. I was no longer frightened, and I rode better than I ever had. It was a wonderful insight into all that I do. The more that I exercised my intent, the more strength I gathered. I even noticed that my physical strength became more acute.

Facing our own death with honor, understanding, and true intent makes death our ally. Having death as an ally helps us out of almost any dangerous situation we might find ourselves in. To give an example, for the warrior, having faced death honorably represents the ultimate power. If you were a gunman in the Old West and were involved in a shoot-out and your intent never wavered, there would be no room for fear; knowing you had done your homework and were the best marksman you could possibly be, death would be your ally. As such a warrior, death would become a guardian and sit on your left shoulder and whisper in your ear, telling you when to move, when to shoot, when to hold back your energy and store it for just the right moment. This becomes a matter of instinct as you bring down spiritual guidance with vertical thought, or reach up toward God. This process focuses your intent, using your endurance, focus, and courage. But this can only happen perfectly when your intent is practiced and well defined, and when your instinct has the freedom to flow. If, for instance, on a more pragmatic level, you have fear of poverty, when you use your intent and get busy making a living, your fear of not having enough will abate. With death as your ally, your life may be saved over and over again, whether literally or metaphorically.

LIVE EVERY MOMENT

Coming from a position of mastery and truthful awareness, from the moment you meet someone you will be aware of the constant possibility of the death of your relationship with that person. Live every moment as if it is your only time together. In fact, it could be. Then every moment becomes precious. This practice creates life as an art form. It will deepen and enrich your relationships.

Sitting with someone who is dying, who has made his or her life an art form, is an enlightening experience. Sitting with those who are unconscious of the magnificence of their own lives is agonizingly different.

Years ago, I was blessed with the experience of being with an extraordinary woman when she chose to pass on. If you have attained personal power and mastery in your life as I have explained it, you will come to the ability of being able to choose when you wish to die; you simply leave your body behind at will when the time is right. The interesting thing about my friend Naomi's death was what she did to prepare. During the several weeks before Naomi died, she traveled the countryside with all of her special belongings in her car. One by one, she gave away the treasures of her life to the people she cared about the most. When she arrived back home, her house was empty except for her bed. Late one afternoon, she called to ask me to come and sit with her, which I was happy to do.

I spent the entire night awake with Naomi, while we lit candles and talked about her life and all that she had done. She spoke about her innermost feelings concerning life, death, and relationships. She told me intimate stories about her husband, who had died many years before. She believed that she was about to join him.

I was rapt listening to her, basking in her love and a kind of radiance that I had never before witnessed in another human being. Her skin was transparent that night; it seemed as thin as tissue paper, with a glow of golden light emanating from within. I knew she had been in pain for many years with cancer, the disease that was about to take her life, and yet it seemed that she was not suffering. It was as if she had already transcended into spirit before releasing her body.

As the sun rose on the horizon, Naomi let go. I held her hand as her spirit left her body, and I felt no tension or resistance whatsoever. A rainbow shone through the window, stretching its colors over her house from one end of town to the other. Naomi had achieved the balance of mastery in her life. She died centered in her personal power with her heart wide open in love. I had the opportunity to be there, to receive the most important teaching of my life: *When we have achieved mastery in our lives, we transform our lives and our health into an experience of complete consciousness of who we are and why we have lived.*

Contrasting this experience, I had occasion to be with a woman named Hilary, who had been dying of heart disease for a long time. I had counseled her during her illness, and she had never been able to embrace the reality that death was imminent. Consequently, she lived her life in terror of the moment when she would step into the unknown. Because she had closed herself to death, her spirit was empty and powerless, and so was her heart. She had never really lived a full life—she had not achieved the balance—and so mastery over her death was not possible.

As I sat with Hilary, she made it clear that directly addressing death in any way was out of the question. Her terror served as a barrier to that kind of intimate communication. All I could do was love her and answer the questions she asked me, even though I saw that it was beyond her to hear the answers. She died a hard death, in heavy resistance and overcome by fear. How could it have been any other way? Death was the last event she wanted to think about, so she had gathered no experience.

BIG DEATHS AND LITTLE DEATHS

Although Hilary's death left me with an overwhelming sadness, she also gave me a very important gift. I saw that each loss or grief that arises in our lives can be treated as a little death. *It is through loss that we may become aware of the spiritual aspects of power as we stand up to our tyrants—our pains and our miseries.* Likewise, it is also through our loss that we may become aware of the spiritual aspects of love, as we struggle to keep our hearts open in the face of pain and fear. Applying the power that we have gathered throughout our lifetime, and offering the love in our open hearts to each little death, will prepare us to die in an expanded state of mastery, blessing all who are lucky enough to be in our presence as we move gracefully from one world into the next.

Not everyone has had the opportunity to be around people

who are dying. Perhaps death is the last thing some of us care to think about. Yet there are indeed all kinds of little deaths in a lifetime—the small deaths when someone loses face or experiences a failure or is in a relationship where the other person leaves. We don't actually die from such experiences, but we may feel as if we are dying. These are small deaths.

Big deaths happen when we literally die on the physical plane (perhaps to be resuscitated, as in a near-death experience). Perhaps we are involved in a serious accident, a misjudgment of action, or someone else's misjudgment of action. In the big deaths of life, we may find ourselves permanently injured or losing everything. We may still be alive, but perhaps we wish we were not. Then power becomes a very different issue. Then, even more than ordinarily, we become aware of the spiritual aspects of mastery. No matter what events occur in your life, each event presents a challenge—a challenge of power, one way or another—and an opening to love.

It is through the challenges of big deaths as well as little deaths that mastery becomes more clearly defined. Through the mirrors of the greater challenges in our lives, we grow more fully.

Sitting with someone who is dying well, someone who has made his or her life into an art form, is an enlightening and uplifting experience. It is, in essence, sitting with a true master. Such a person models for us how to face our own deaths—large and small—as well as how to make our final exits from our physical bodies with grace and power. When we at last view death as our final act of power, performed with an open heart, we can move that understanding throughout our lives. When we achieve our goal of being present and aware, we have finally perfected the balance between love and power. In complete acceptance of life, death, and all that comes between, we become masters of our own destinies.

Ideas to Contemplate

1. Am I afraid of death? Why?

2. How do my thoughts about death influence my life?

3. If I could design my death, how would I see it?

4. Is my intent strong and focused? List the ways it is strong.

5. When am I afraid?

6. How could I strengthen my intent to enable me to wipe away my fear?

13

Life Is Like a Clay Pot

It feels as though I make my way
through massive rock
like a vein of ore
alone, encased.
I am so deep inside it
I can't see the path or any distance:
everything is close
and everything closing in on me
has turned to stone.

Since I still don't know enough
about pain,
this terrible darkness makes me
small.
If it's you, though—
press down hard on me, break in
that I may know the weight of your
hand,
and you, the fullness of my cry.

—Rainer Maria Rilke

There is an image that I have held close to me over the years, one that comforted my soul in a deep way. I'd like to share it with you.

As a young girl, I was in the wilderness of eastern Washington State, riding my pinto pony, Sugar. I was following a slow-moving creek in search of what we called soapstone. We usually found it just under the surface of the water. I was riding in a deep canyon that day surrounded by high cliffs of granite. As I rounded a corner in the creek, I saw up ahead the silhouette of the most beautiful woman. I stopped, and Sugar's ears pricked intently forward, also watching. I did not want to disturb her. She was Native American. Her long black hair flowed like liquid obsidian down her back. Her red cotton dress was beaded in the old style. She was bending over the sparkling creek and gathering water into a large clay pot. When it was sufficiently full, she straightened up and placed the pot on her head, still balancing it with both hands. She gracefully walked away from me down the trail and out of sight. Sugar snorted and whinnied softly. I never saw her again. But the memory of that somehow startling moment that seemed out of time and place has always stayed with me. In thinking about it, I felt so deeply the simple beauty of life. The woman represented such grace and power in the way she expertly scooped the water from the creek. The clay pot seemed like our life-form, held in beauty and ever filled with the flow of eternity. This was a very special moment I shall never forget because it taught me a new way of seeing.

I began to look at my life as a form—a kind of clay pot—something that I was trying to create and develop as part of the process of defining my soul, but also something substantial that has a limitation, a boundary, a definition. You, too, might begin to think of your life as a clay pot. In your imagination, form your clay pot as beautifully as you possibly can. Make it smooth, rounded, and carefully crafted.

When you think of your life as a clay pot, you think of it as having a reason for being, a purpose, and you take it and fill it with your experience. You fill it with everything from harmony to disharmony. Like all vessels that contain things, it must also be emptied from time to time so that you can fill it with new things, new experiences. The emptying offers one extraordinary experience—the experience of letting go, of release, and of giving away, often in a sacred way, sometimes with great pain, as when you let go of what no longer serves you.

Emptying the pot is the antithesis of the filling, the gathering, the collecting, the compiling of energies that go into filling the clay pot, but it is equally essential to your process of growth and makes possible the gathering of new energies.

Where in all the experience of form and limitation is the place, that moment of perfection, where mastery is present? There is the art with which one looks at life and uses one's ability to create, which is an essential component of mastery. There are the techniques of our trade—our degrees, study, and practice that we spend years and years learning—that are also a part of mastery. But at some point, with all of this filling up of the pot, there comes a time when the emptying is necessary if anything more is to be obtained. At some point you are filled. There is no more room. At such a point, we face a moment, a place of power, a time of growing, which I call a crossroads, where a choice has to be made.

The essence of you as a clay pot is an energy form moving constantly like a pot on the potter's wheel, and you fill your vessel with other energy forms moving at different rates of power and strength and light. When you are filling the vessel that is you, you are imploding energy, or taking energy into you through knowledge and practice. Though we live in a male-dominated world, the filling of the clay pot represents the female, receptive mode. At some point, there has to be explosion, an opposite and equal reaction, which is the male mode. And so the emptying begins. This is a very different energy flow. Instead of taking in, you are giving out. The energy is flowing out of you like water over a dam, flowing out of you into other energy fields, perhaps lost to you forever, and yet still part of you forever. But there is more.

A moment after these choices have been made, when you have chosen to let go of old relationships and ideas that hold you back, for example, there comes a crossroads in your experience as a person of power. *Just before the moment when the flow begins in the opposite direction—the flow of letting go and release—there comes a superior moment in your life. A moment is visited upon you like no other. It is a moment of stillness, when you*

wait, and you listen, and you feel the essence of your creation as
you stay aware—the essence of your god.

If you are experienced enough and have an open heart, if you
know the components of love and can feel the total balance
between implosion and explosion before actual movement
begins, then perhaps the essence of mastery will join you for a
short conversation, and you will feel the balance of power. You
could have a dialogue about truth and life, and about your feelings of worth and whether the course of your life matters or not.
You will sense the importance of your point of view and whether
that point of view is necessary to continue in your life.

You come face-to-face with the magnificent specter of death
and life and the mirror that it creates. In looking into that mirror, you come to realize whether your life is successful or not.
In that mirror, if mastery has not yet been created in your life,
new images begin to develop and perhaps the kind of enlightenment that is mastery, that kind of ecstatic experience, will come
into you. This moment is truly a dialogue with the infinite.
Symbolically, it is a dialogue with the essence of the clay pot that
you are. You know that you are limited by your form, and yet
you are one with all other forms so that there is no separation, a
seemingly contradictory state. There is only a oneness of all
existence.

This realization of oneness is part of the process of mastery,
because in mastery there is an understanding of when to hold
on and when to let go, when to feel separation, when to learn
from it, and when to melt into oneness. If this part of the gathering and filling of the clay pot comes, then the decision naturally
follows to separate yourself from all of these experiences with
new perspective and allow them to flow out of you like the
breath of God. You are at one with that breath. It isn't what you
fill the pot with, or the process of emptying the pot, but the idea
that somewhere at the crossroads, as you make your choice,

enlightenment comes. You begin to understand that it is the emptiness of that magnificent clay pot, the clay pot which is you, the beautiful space that you are, that represents the fullness of your life and your capacity for mastery.

Ideas to Contemplate

1. How do you define your structure in life—what you have metaphorically called your clay pot?

2. Have you ever reached a crossroads in your life where stillness occurs? What happened? What choices did you make?

3. Have you pulled in (imploded) energy in your life? How?

4. Have you expressed energy (exploded) in your life? How?

5. Write a prayer of gratefulness for all that you are.

6. Have you experienced moments of mastery? Describe them.

Epilogue:
An Opening

Fools believe that knowing brings them power
Such power-knowing is just another hollow
The only real knowing is Loving, for when
Mystery begins, only Love can follow.

—ANDREW HARVEY, LOVE'S GLORY: RE-CREATIONS OF RUMI

There are times when I have a vision of my God and I know why I am alive. This happens to me most often at sunset as I watch the play of light across the sky, the crimson and peach clouds edged with golden light from the setting sun. I feel my existence reflected in that light, and I know I have a purpose in this lifetime. Even if I have doubts and fears at moments, I know that somehow there has been a silver cord pulling me toward my destiny. When I sit in a place of stillness, with my head leaning against a rock in the vast wilderness of southern Arizona, and I allow myself to stop speaking and to rest and to dream, I feel my heart opening; I feel it throughout my entire body. My mind takes a rest, and I realize that the possibility of a truly balanced, harmonious, almost God-like life is truly accessible.

Mastery is at hand if we just open ourselves to the possibility. But most of us fall prey to our conditioning and our human- ness—which is most likely about "what we are supposed to do." Overcoming our failings and our difficulties is part of why we are here on earth. But it's always in the stillness that the world of the Great Spirit, of God, of the great Goddess presence on this earth, comes into me. I realize that we are in an angelic realm, that we are protected, in a way, because we are supposed to evolve into the new millennium, great soaring creatures who understand the balance of nature and spirit and physicality. Oftentimes, I think about acts of power, reaching up for divine inspiration in vertical consciousness, and I move into that place of experience with my apprentices where they express their acts of intent and realize their shortcomings and their tremendous strengths. Reflected in their beautiful shining faces, I see the radiance of God—that is my students' gift to me as their teacher.

Once again, it is in the stillness that this truth is found. But oftentimes, it is within the action, too. It is within the move- ment out into the world. Imagine a football player running for a touchdown, running as fast as he can, and suddenly he has the sense of running in slow motion, almost as if he is running above himself, looking down at himself. I have spoken to many athletes who have had this experience.

Again, it is within the stillness of action that these moments of clarity occur when you see your place within the scheme of things. You see the reason for your birth and the reason for your death. *You understand that death is an ally, that you only have a few moments, a blink of an eye, in this lifetime to learn what you came here to learn.* In death—whatever that means to you, whether it is a long sleep, a meeting with your maker, a time of judgment, a time of reckoning—it is a time of change, when, certainly, there is a reckoning within your own consciousness of what you have accomplished in this life and what you have left behind. You only take your experience and what I call the "sacred witness" with you. The sacred witness is that place of quietude within your own soul where you look out upon the world from a place of strength and power, and you balance spirit with the physical, art and passion with technique. You direct yourself homeward to a place of mastery. It is at this time that you realize that all is possible and that within your own imagination lie the greatest dreams of creation.

I live my life in widening rings
which spread over earth and sky.
I may not ever complete the last one,
but that is what I will try.
I circle around God, the primordial tower,
and I circle ten thousand years long;
and I still don't know if I'm a falcon, a storm,
or an unfinished poem.

—Rainer Maria Rilke

ENTER A COSMOLOGY OF MYSTERY, MAGIC, AND POWER WITH LYNN ANDREWS

For the last ten years I have been describing my learning and my path. It has been a joy to do this. In continuing my journey, I would be grateful if you would share your insights with me.

In addition, you are invited to join me at my June retreat in the high Mojave desert for four days of ceremony, sacred community, meditation, and healing. Please call or write for scheduled dates and detailed information. In addition, expanded in-depth training is available at the Lynn Andrews Center for Arts and Training beginning each February. Also available are over twenty audiotapes, beautifully produced and digitally recorded, including guided meditations and a very special selection of teachings, personal reflections, and sacred music.

Please send me your name and address so that I can share any new information with you:

Lynn Andrews
2934½ Beverly Glen Circle
Box 378
Los Angeles, CA 90077
1–800–726–0082
www.lynnandrews.com